THE
GOLF SWING

CARY MIDDLECOFF

edited by Tom Michael

BURFORD BOOKS

Library of Congress Cataloging-in-Publication Data
Middlecoff, Cary.
    The golf swing / Cary Middlecoff ; edited by Tom Michael.
        p.   cm.
    Originally published: Englewood Cliffs, NJ ; Prentice-Hall, 1974.
    ISBN 1-58080-074-2 (pbk.)
    1. Swing (Golf).   I. Michael, Tom.   II. Title.
GV979.S9M52   1999
796.352'3—dc21   *98-51038*
                                                   CIP

Introduction
to the 1999 Edition

If you are a student of the golf swing, your personal library must include a copy of Dr. Cary Middlecoff's *The Golf Swing*. This book describes and articulates the top professional swings from the wooden-shaft era of Harry Vardon through the Arnold Palmer/Jack Nicklaus era of the 1970's. These top-playing professionals' swings are analyzed and discussed in detail. *The Golf Swing* is the best chronicle of the golf swing developed during this time period and is accompanied by photographs appropriate to the era of each player.

The preface to *The Golf Swing* states, "the golf swing is an evolving process. The techniques in use today [1960's and 1970's] are basically the product of study and experimentation." These players developed their swing techniques as a result of personal feel and with help and observations from their fellow touring professionals.

The professional touring players of today, however, developed their swings in a very different manner. Most of today's players had professional instruction in the early stages of their careers. This early instruction was followed by professional coaching and swing development augmented by high-speed video photography.

The use of modern video and computer imagery changed the player's development from what the swing *feels* like to what the swing *looks* like in high-speed, slow-motion film. Today's coach constantly monitors the swing of the playing professional. The player's swing is continuously revised to keep it at its highest level of proficiency. Changes that occur naturally in the swing are monitored and the revisions are checked.

The 1990's tour professional's golf swing is developed to maximize use of the player's physical skills. Today's professionals also work with personal trainers to improve and maintain their physical and mental skill levels. This is a dramatic change from earlier years. So golf development has changed from the modeling-driven era of Dr. Middlecoff to the video-driven era of contemporary tour professionals.

The pictures and narrative in *The Golf Swing* make clear that there are great players of all physical types, each with his personal swing style. The overriding value which all players show is this—the swing they have developed fits their particular physical abilities and personality style.

As a player, you should evaluate your physical abilities and the type of playing style that fits your personality. Study players of similar size and abilities for specific traits that you can copy. Likewise, be aware of styles that do not fit your abilities.

Contrast the swings of these past champions to the swings of today's players as you watch them perform. Notice that the swings of today's professionals are more mechanically uniform than the individual styles of previous champions—again the result of learning the swing by stop-action video rather than by feel.

There are techniques to learn from every great player, but not all these techniques are right for you. Work with your coach to develop the best traits for your individual golf game.

—Rick Martino
PGA Master Professional
Director of Instruction, Professional Golfers
Association of America

Preface

The golf swing is an evolving process—the techniques in successful use today are basically the product of study and experimentation carried out in the past and handed down through precept and example. It is a process that had its beginning when golf was first played (some three to four centuries ago, according to most historians), and it will probably continue for as long as the game is played. Thus it follows that the golfer who aspires to understand and use the best modern methods should have some knowledge of how they came about.

Over a hundred years ago a leading Scottish professional and clubmaker named Daniel A. Forgan said of golf, "It is a science —the study of a lifetime in which you may exhaust yourself but never your subject." In our own era, the great Ben Hogan said, "Every year we learn a little more about golf. Each chunk of valid knowledge paves the way to greater knowledge. Golf is like medicine and the other fields of science in this respect. In another fifteen years, just as there will be many new discoveries in medicine based on and made possible by present-day strides, we will similarly have refined and extended our present-day knowledge of golf."

It seems clear, then, that a study of golf techniques can be both endlessly interesting and highly rewarding in terms of lower scores and therefore greater enjoyment of the game. The key to accomplishing this, of course, is to know as much as you can about hitting a golf ball correctly. Then the learning process can be continued on the highest possible level.

There are two main ways to learn golf. One is by observing good players in action and adapting various principles and features of their swings to yours. The other is by taking lessons from a competent professional. Note that I do not include reading instructional books among the basic ways to learn the game—but I do regard books as a means of augmenting and speeding up the learning process. Good instruction books enable you to understand what you see when you observe good players or what your professional tells you and shows you on the lesson tee. A major drawback to learning by reading is that the various books (more than three thousand have been published since 1857) contain so many statements that are, or seem to be, contradictory. You find, for instance, one authority (Harry Vardon) saying that the club should be gripped firmly with the thumb and forefinger of the right hand, and another (Ben Hogan) saying that gripping firmly with these two fingers is a "swing-wrecker."

In tracing the development of the modern golf swing, we will present a number of these contradictions and paradoxes, reconcile them where possible, and examine them in light of methods and techniques that are presently enjoying the greatest success. After studying some of the great swings of the past, we will look closely at the swings of some twenty leading players on the Professional Golfers Association Tour—players who can be seen at tournaments around the country and who appear with some regularity on television.

It strikes me that beginning golfers nowadays have a considerable advantage over those of just a decade or so ago. They can watch and study the world's best golfers in action either in person at a tournament in their particular section of the country, or on television. In this way, they can know from the start what a good golf swing looks like. Also, they can see that while all good golf swings do not look alike superficially, certain fundamental techniques are common to all.

When the touring professionals came only to a few cities, and before television was sufficiently improved technically to allow the watcher a clear view of the players in action, beginning golfers often modeled their swings on that of a single player— usually the best one in their area. That player's swing may have been good and fundamentally sound, fully worthy of emulation, but in some cases it wasn't. In any case the aspiring beginner may have been looking at the wrong things—the superficialities rather than the basics. Furthermore, the beginner couldn't be sure that he had the right model. He might keep it in the back of his mind that he could get a lot better if he could see and study the swing of, say, Jones or Hagen or Hogan or Nelson or Snead.

I was exceptionally fortunate that my original model was a great Memphis amateur named Emmett Spicer. Right from the beginning—this was in the early 1930s—I considered Spicer's way of hitting a golf ball basically correct. His was a graceful, easy style, and he hit the ball as well as any player I have seen since. Even so, I wondered about Jones and Hagen and the other greats of that period. (I later learned that I could have had no better model than Spicer.) Incidentally, none of my friends ever saw any great similarity between Spicer's swing and mine.

The fact is that I did not try to make my swing look like Spicer's, or anybody else's, but I tried to incorporate into my swing what I took to be the fundamental positions and movements that made Spicer's swing produce such powerful and accurate shots. That, I still think, is the approach that all aspiring golfers should take.

Contents

Vardon's Part

If you had to designate one person as the "father of the modern golf swing," the most logical choice would be Harry Vardon. There were renowned golfers before Vardon first came to prominence late in the nineteenth century, but none of them captured the imagination of the golfing public as he did. Vardon won the British Open—then the premier tournament in the world of golf—six times between 1896 and 1911. He won the United States Open in 1900, and was in that historic playoff for the United States Open in 1913 won by the then twenty-year-old Francis Ouimet at The Country Club in Brookline, Massachusetts. This epochal event is rightly credited with giving golf its first great wave of popularity on an international scale. In addition, Vardon played a series of exhibition matches in the United States in 1900 and thus was seen in action by golf enthusiasts in various sections of the nation.

Harry Vardon at Baltusrol Golf Club, Springfield, N.J. (1913).

In addition to being considered the best golfer of his era, Vardon had grace and style plus that largely indefinable quality now known as "color." Most of those who watched him play became convinced that a golf swing was good to whatever extent it resembled Vardon's, and wrong to whatever extent it didn't. Therefore the Vardon swing was widely imitated in the United States, as was already the case in Great Britain. (By way of illustrating the evolutionary aspect of golf techniques, it should be noted that Robert T. Jones, Jr., saw Vardon play in Atlanta when Jones was at the impressionable age of eleven and, as he later said, was tremendously influenced by what he saw. A few years later, of course, it was the Jones swing that came to be the model for golfers everywhere, and his influence remains strongly in effect even today.)

It having been more than fifty years since Vardon was last on the competitve golf scene, there are very few golfers who know anything about his methods from personal experience. Therefore, we must turn to the instructional books that he authored (or coauthored) to learn what his theories were and how he developed them. Vardon wrote some half-dozen books. In at least one of them his coauthor was Bernard Darwin, the foremost golf writer of his day and a personal friend of Vardon. Of perhaps greater importance, Darwin was himself one of the best amateur golfers in Great Britain— good enough to have represented his country in international competition for more than twenty years. It may be assumed, then, that the Vardon-Darwin book most accurately presented Vardon's thought on how to hit a golf ball.

Like virtually all golfers before or since who tried to impart their own knowledge of golf to others, Vardon put primary emphasis on the grip. As just about every golfer in the world knows, the grip in basic use today is called the Vardon grip. In his day, the Vardon grip was a radical departure from that used by earlier golfers of note, most of whom, as early golf photographs show, wrapped both thumbs around the shaft and essentially held the club in the palms rather than the fingers. The Vardon changes included gripping the club more in the fingers than the palms, putting the left thumb down the top of the shaft rather than around it, and overlapping the index finger of the left hand with the little finger of the right. It is this latter refinement that distinguishes the Vardon grip from the interlocking grip and the ten-finger grip, which also have been successfully used in modern times.

In the interlocking grip, the index finger of the left hand and the little finger of the right are, as the name indicates, interlocked instead of overlapped. In the ten-finger grip, all

Harry Vardon, 1922, at the Bellevue Golf Club, Syracuse, New York.

A good view of the famous Vardon Grip in action during a round of the
920 National Open Golf Tournament at Inverness Country Club.

fingers of both hands are on the shaft. (This grip is often erroneously called the baseball grip, although it is as essentially different from the grip used on a baseball bat as are the overlapping and interlocking grips.) The interlocking and ten-finger grips simply represent slight and allowable personal modifications of what is called the Vardon (or overlapping) grip. Proof is in the fact that Jack Nicklaus and, in a slightly earlier era, Lloyd Mangrum, have done wonderfully well with the interlocking grip. And, with respect to the ten-finger grip, it has served very well for Art Wall, Jr., and Bob Rosburg.

Vardon said that he experimented continually for more than a year before settling on the grip that was to bear his name. As to its suitability for others, he noted that he had very large hands with long, thick fingers, and added that his was a problem of "finding room on the club" for his hands. He thus implied that golfers with smaller hands, as exemplified in particular by Wall and Rosburg, might not need to overlap one finger with another.

Curiously—or so it seems now—Vardon stated that he applied the strongest grip pressure with the thumb and index finger of each hand and deliberately loosened the last three fingers of the left hand at the top of the backswing. Later golfers and golf theorists, notably Ben Hogan, emphasized that both these points were quite wrong, that the main pressure should be in the middle two fingers of the right hand and the last three fingers of the left, with the barest minimum of pressure applied by the thumb and index finger of the right hand. And it is now generally and fully accepted that there must be no loosening of the grip at the top of the backswing or at any other stage of the swing.

In this we see the process of evolution, so to speak, at work in golf methods and techniques. Golfers are still experimenting with the grip. Their conclusions will be presented later on in this book. At this point, it is sufficient to point out that all of the modern theorists began their experimentation with the basic Vardon grip, or some slight variation of it.

Vardon laid the groundwork. Even if he was wrong on a couple of points, as it now appears, the fact remains that his contributions to the science (or art) of golf were tremendous.

From reading his books, it seems also that he made a contribution of another sort by showing how hard it can be to transfer thoughts on golf to other persons through the spoken or written word. Even with so competent a collaborator as Bernard Darwin, he stated things that he couldn't possibly have meant. For conspicuous example, he said that "at impact the weight should be equally distributed on both feet," and the position at impact "should be in all respects the same as it was at the start of the swing." Yet action pictures of him clearly show that, like all good golfers, he began to shift the bulk of his weight to the left side at the beginning of the downswing, and at impact his hips had moved well forward of their original position. And certainly he made no backward movement during the downswing that would equalize weight distribution at impact. This is surely one of those bits of misunderstanding that can creep in when one man tries to impart to another what he feels and senses while in the act of hitting a golf ball.

Incidentally, I should perhaps admit that Vardon indirectly took a pretty good dig at my swing in his writings—even though it was to be several years after his death before I first picked up a golf club. "Do not dwell," wrote Vardon, with heavy emphasis, meaning that there should be no perceptible pause between the end of the backswing and the start of the downswing. Well, I dwelt. No question about that. I'm sure that in my prime I dwelt longer at the top of the backswing than any other successful golfer ever did. And I have been told that my best days on the course were marked by pauses even longer than usual.

I do not argue the point with Vardon, or his ghost. I think it shows that there are many personal modifications in all effective golf swings, even though the fundamentals are constant.

In the matter of stance, Vardon held that the toes of both feet should be turned "well outward." He said that this facilitated the hip turn, or pivot, on the backswing, and made for greater freedom of body and arm movement on the downswing. Vardon's precepts about the positioning of the feet remained orthodox until Hogan came along with the positive assertion that the right foot should be squared (at right angles with the intended line of flight) and the left foot only should be turned outward. As we shall see, Hogan felt that the lower body turn on the backswing should be restricted rather than emphasized, and that the squared right foot acted as a sort of governor on the amount of turn the hips could and should take. (Vardon, of course, always played in a rather tight-fitting sports jacket, as did his contemporaries, and it may have been that they needed the right foot turned outward to enable them to take even a minimum body turn on the backswing.) At any rate, the modern trend is toward the right foot squared and the left turned outward.

Vardon advocated, as have all golf theorists, that both knees should be flexed at the start of the stroke. But, said Vardon, "The right leg stiffens . . . until at the top of the backswing it is quite rigid." And he advocated the same stiffening process for the left leg on the downswing. These notions persisted for many years, particularly with regard to the left leg, as indicated by the continuing advocacy of "hitting against a firm left side." (In 1898, one H. R. Sweny wrote a book called *Keep Your Eye on the Ball and Your Right Knee Stiff*, and the text showed that he considered these the true keys to good golf.)

Vardon seems to have been the first expert to discount the theory of the "wrist snap" in producing powerful shots. Vardon wrote:

> Now pay attention to the wrists. They should be held fairly tightly. If the club is held tightly the wrists will be tight, and vice versa. When the wrists are tight there is little play in them, and more is demanded of the arms. I don't believe in the long ball coming from the

wrists. In defiance of principles which are accepted in many quarters [author's note: and still are] I will go so far as to say that, except in putting, there is no pure wrist shot in golf. Some players attempt to play their short approaches with their wrists as they have been told to do. These men are likely to remain at long handicaps for a long time. Similarly there is a kind of superstition that the elect among drivers get in some peculiar kind of "snap"—a momentary forward pushing movement—with their wrists at the time of impact, and that it is this wrist work at the critical period which gives the grand length to their drives, those extra twenty or thirty yards which make the stroke look so splendid, so uncommon, and which make the next shot so much easier. Generally speaking, the wrists when held firmly will take very good care of themselves. . . .

Had Vardon succeeded in getting this point across with sufficient force, it probably would have amounted to as great a contribution to better golf as had the Vardon grip. But many golfers—a considerable majority, I think—still cling to the notion of a wrist snap being the source of the extra power that the better golfers get. You hear such expressions as "he really gets his wrists into the shot." It perhaps would be more accurate to say of a good golfer that "he sure manages to keep his wrists out of the shot."

Another point that Vardon made needs to be brought out because it will relate directly to our subsequent discussion of what Ben Hogan called his "secret." Said Vardon:

From the moment when the club is first taken back, the left wrist should begin to turn inwards (that is to say, the movement is in the same direction as that taken by the hands of a clock), and so turn away the face of the club from the ball. When this is properly done, the toe of the club will point to the sky when it is level with the shoulder and will be dead over the middle of the shaft. This turning or twisting process continues all the way until at the top of the swing the toe of the club is pointing straight downwards to the ground.

This clockwise turning or twisting of the wrists and hands on the backswing later came to be known as pronation (Vardon did not use the term). For the record, "pronation" is defined as "a medial rotation of the hand and radius around the ulna so that the palm is turned backward or downward; also the position resulting from this movement—opposed to supination." As to "supination," another term that came to be used with some frequency in golf instruction, it is simply the opposite of "pronation.")

Although Vardon set the standard for his era, he was not without keen rivals in Great Britain. He, J. H. Taylor, and James Braid came to be known as The Triumvirate, in much the same way as, in recent years, Arnold Palmer, Jack Nicklaus, and Gary Player came to be called The Big Three. Taylor and Braid, whose ages were within a year of Vardon's each won the British Open five times. Taylor was described as having "a peculiar, flat-footed style." Braid was said to give the ball "a sudden, furious lash." Both are doubtless excellent and colorful golfers, but neither's method of striking the ball had the wide appeal to the public that Vardon's did. Also, Taylor and Braid were little-known in the United States, which made it easy for Vardon to become the idol and model of golfers on both sides of the Atlantic.

No golfer has ever been totally without his critics and detractors. Taylor said that Vardon lifted the club too abruptly at the start of the backswing. Darwin, his collaborator, said Vardon's swing could be improved by keeping the right elbow closer to the body instead of letting it "wander at will," and agreed with Taylor about the too pronounced lift of the club on the backswing. But Vardon had the good sense to stay aloof from such arguments, and the vast majority of golfers kept on believing that the Vardon way was *the* way. This view was to be generally held until Robert T. Jones of Atlanta became the international hero and idol of golf.

The
One and Only
Bobby

It has now been forty years since Bobby Jones bestrode the world of golf as did no other before. Arnold Palmer was in his first year of life when Jones was performing the last of those incredible feats that gave him his unique and exalted place in the annals of the game—and which, more to the point, made aspiring golfers all over the world want to swing the golf club as he did. Therefore, for younger golfers in particular, it may be necessary to review enough of his career to explain how he so completely captured the admiration and imagination of the world of golf that all the champions before him (and his contemporaries as well) were all but forgotten or ignored.

Most golfers even today can tell you that in 1930 Jones won what came to be known as golf's Grand Slam, and that the term means winning in a single year the United States

Bobby Jones getting out of sand during practice round for the National Open(1930).

Open, the British Open, the United States Amateur, and the British Amateur. There was, of course, no Masters tournament then, and as an amateur Jones could not compete in the P.G.A. championship. So he had won in one year every top honor in golf open to him.

Not so well-known are prior facts about Jones's career that to many discerning golfers—including Jones himself—are at least as impressive as his Grand Slam. In the last nine years of his career, from age twenty to age twenty-eight, he played in nine United States Opens and three British Opens and finished either first or second in nine of those tournaments. And in the last seven of those nine years, he won thirteen major national championships. Add to this that in retiring as a competitor at twenty-eight, he left to the public's imagination just what heights of greatness he might have achieved had he played on through his prime. He had personality, wit, style—all the qualities that make an athlete popular both with spectators and fellow competitors. Consider that he, an amateur, consistently beat the game's professionals for a full decade and yet kept their friendship and admiration. Consider also that, as an American, he was the idol of British galleries during all the years that he was humbling that nation's champions. That was Jones—Bobby to the press and public, Bob to his friends.

Having basically established what Jones did in golf, we come to the question of the methods and techniques he used to do it, and how he so greatly influenced golfers of his day and afterward.

Jones wrote no comprehensive instructional material during his playing career. Also, there was surprisingly little effort on the part of others to analyze his swing in depth and point out just what made it so spectacularly effective. Golf writers of his day mostly recorded his deeds. When reference was made to his swing, the writers applied such adjectives as "perfect," "flawless," "fluid," "flowing," "graceful," and the like. And, of course, there was no television to permit showing his swing to the millions, with slow motion, stop-action, and analytical

The great Bobby Jones on his way to the Grand Slam of golf at the Merion Cricket Club, Ardmore, Pennsylvania, in the National Amateur Golf Championship (1930).

commentary. Had there been, I feel certain that the average level of golf ability would have risen considerably more than it did in the 1920s and 1930s.

Some of the writers of his day likened Jones to a "mechanical man," implying that his brilliant game came automatically and with almost no effort on his part. Jones did not agree. He said that he rarely had full confidence in his swing, and he attributed much of his success to his competitive instincts— his ability to rise to the occasion and play his best golf when it was most desperately needed—rather than to an unvarying, automatic, mechanical swing. There is reason to believe that part of the reason for his early retirement was his awareness that it would take time and work for him to stay on top in golf, more time and work than he felt he should give at that stage in his life.

After retirement from tournament competition, Jones made a series of instructional films in Hollywood. Only then could his swing be studied by the millions instead of the thousands privileged to see him in person during his tournament career. These short films were far and away the most popular things of their kind ever done, and the Jones influence on the public concept of what a golf swing should look like was considerably enhanced.

A few years later, Jones wrote a book called *Golf Is My Game*, in which the first eighty pages were devoted to his views on the technical aspects of hitting a golf ball. At the outset, Jones revealed some of the major steps in developing his own game. He said, for instance, that he took no formal lessons but took as his basic model the swing of Stewart Maiden, the professional at the East Lake Club in Atlanta where Jones's father was a member, and where, at the age of seven or eight, Jones first began to play on a full-sized course. Jones said that at first he tried to swing as nearly as possible as Maiden did, but soon set about to develop his own style based on the fundamental movements he discerned in Maiden's swing. He disdained conscious imitation of another's style and realized that he would have to work out his own problems if he was to fulfill his youthful ambition to play golf on the championship level.

It is rare that any writer of a how-to golf book begins other than with a discussion of the correct grip. Jones did. He theorized that an aspiring golfer should first and most importantly learn how the clubface and the ball interact when contact is made between the two.

"Golf is played by striking the ball with the head of the club," Jones wrote, emphasizing an obvious fact much as other golf writers begin by stating that the grip represents the only connection between the player and the club.

> *The objective of the player is not to swing the club in a specified manner, nor to execute a series of complicated movements in a prescribed sequence, nor to look pretty while he is doing it, but primarily and essentially to strike the ball with the head of the club so that the ball will perform according to his wishes.*
>
> *No one can play golf until he knows the many ways in which a golf ball can be expected to respond when it is struck in different ways. If you think that all this should be obvious, please believe me when I assure you that I have seen many really good players attempt shots they should have known were impossible.*

Jones, who learned engineering principles at Georgia Tech before going through Harvard Law School, produced a number of drawings to show how underspin is produced by a downward blow in which the clubface makes initial contact with the lower part of the ball, how left-to-right spin is produced by bringing the clubface across the ball from right to left, and how right-to-left spin is produced by compressing the ball on the side nearest the player. Said Jones:

> *As a practical matter, it is not possible to slide the face of the club across the ball from left to right (inside to outside the line), but the mere fact that the back of the ball has been compressed on the side nearest the player will cause it to spin in a counterclockwise direction and therefore to hook.*

*If you have ever been told that the clubhead should
strike the ball while traveling from inside the line of flight
to the outside, forget it. This advice may have been of
temporary helpfulness on occasion when the player, in at-
tempting to follow it, has corrected a natural tendency to
hit across the ball from the outside. But the player who
actually succeeds in hitting from the inside-to-out more
often finds himself plagued by a ducking hook.*

In discussing the grip, Jones generally accepted what
Vardon had said, but he had different ideas about how much
pressure should be applied and where it should be principally
concentrated. "A tight grip necessarily tenses all of the
muscles and tendons of the wrists and forearms so that any
degree of flexibility is impossible," said Jones. Also, contrary
to Vardon's dictums, Jones said that the club should be held
mainly by the last three fingers of the left hand—not, as
Vardon prescribed, mainly by the thumb and index finger of
each hand.

Jones also was as strong for keeping the wrists flexible as
Vardon was for keeping them "tight" and "firm." Jones made
repeated use of the word "gentle" in describing how much
overall pressure should be applied in the grip. All these descriptive terms are, of course, relative, and there is no sure
way of knowing just how much Jones and Vardon differed
in their respective theories of how tightly or gently the club
should be held. Nevertheless, there does appear to be a considerable divergence of opinion on the subject between these
two superexponents of the game. The answer would seem to
be that there is considerable latitude for the individual golfer
to work out his own solution to the problem. Perhaps he
should say that he mustn't squeeze the club and neither
should he hold it so loosely as not to have it under control.

Among the privileges I have enjoyed through golf is that
of having played with Jones some twenty or thirty times just
after World War II when I was an Army dental officer
stationed at Augusta, Georgia, and Jones had been discharged

after his own service in that war. This was in 1946, the year before I turned professional, and about two years before Jones began having the serious physical problems that were to deny him the pleasure of playing the game he so greatly enjoyed and at which he had so long excelled. Jones was not then the golfer he had been. But he still retained essentially the same fluid swing that had made him so great. He did not, of course, have the old competitive fire and concentration, but the physical elements were still present and clearly recognizable.

One of the first things I noticed was that Jones's style seemed totally natural. He stood to the ball with rather a narrower stance than most good golfers use, his knees turned slightly inward toward each other and his weight more to the inside of his feet than the outside. This also was the way he stood and walked. It has been established that the inside muscles of the legs (and arms) are the ones that should dominate to produce a good golf swing, which for Jones was perfectly natural.

I noticed also that his wrists seemed more than ordinarily flexible—which made it easy and natural for him to take a long backswing with the club shaft dipping well below the horizontal at the top—on all shots from the woods down through the medium irons. Additionally, he could take a very full turn of the hips and shoulders with no apparent strain whatever—all ease and grace. Jones was then in his mid-forties, and it was easy to picture what his swing had been like when he was in his twenties. It took no great insight to understand why his was the style that other golfers wanted to copy.

The things I saw as chiefly characterizing his swing were the things that later in writing he set forth as the correct elements of the golf stroke. As for his relatively narrow stance, it should be noted that because he naturally kept his weight to the inside of his feet, he had no need to spread his feet wider apart to maintain balance.

The Jones grip differed in one detail from the grip most favored by today's top golfers. He put his left hand on the club in what is called a strong position, meaning that it was turned back to the right so that in looking straight down from the position of address he could see the first three knuckles of the left hand. This was considered standard for many years, but in the so-called modern grip the left hand is turned more around to the left so that the back of the hand is faced more toward the target. The strong position of the left hand tends to promote a hook and is in fact used by today's best golfers when they want to hook the ball deliberately. In this connection, I particularly remember that Jones told me he went through the Grand Slam year of 1930 allowing for a slight hook on every full shot he hit. "I would just line up 10 yards or so to the right of the target and swing naturally," Jones recalled, "and feel confident that that little hook would be there to bring it in where I wanted it." There is no way to know, of course, whether Jones would have changed his grip had he continued to play. I do know that he was strongly against trying to correct swing faults by altering the grip.

A much-needed tip that Jones gave me back in 1947 reveals his own theory of the approach to the ball and the preliminary swing movements known as the waggle. My problem centered on the fact that I would take my stance, begin to waggle the club and sight the target, and then just get frozen over the ball. I couldn't seem to make the transition from the waggle into the backswing. After a time, Jones suggested that I predetermine to start by backswing on a certain count and force myself to do so regardless of whether I felt myself ready. From this, and by observation, I learned that Jones began his swing by means of a rhythmic pattern that involved a count. He would begin his approach to the ball from a few steps behind it, in line with the target, meanwhile settling himself into the smooth movement he wanted for the execution of the shot. Then he would plant first the right foot and then the left, combine a slight forward press with a single waggle of the club, and go quickly yet smoothly into the backswing. It seemed to go on a count of one, two, three, swing. (The count I adopted as a result of his advice was rather more protracted but similar in principle, and it helped me a lot.)

Jones described his backswing as "moderately flat," and he was strongly against pronating the left wrist.

> Many players begin the backswing with a sudden pronation of the left wrist that whips the club sharply around the legs, opening the clubface very quickly. This is just as bad as a swing straight back (upright), carrying the arms away from the body.
>
> The initial movement of the club away from the ball should result from forces originating in the left side. The real takeoff is from the left foot, starting the movement of the body. The hands and arms soon pick it up, but the proper order at the very beginning is body, arms, and lastly clubhead. It is always easier to continue a motion than to begin it; this order has the virtue of originating the hip turn; it goes a long way toward assuring a proper windup of the hips during the backswing.

(We shall see in the following section that Ben Hogan's ideas on starting the backswing are, at least on the surface, at considerable variance with those of Jones. As to the proper order of movement at the beginning, Hogan said it was hands, shoulders, hips, but noted that these movements should be so nearly simultaneous that the average golfer should think of them that way.)

There is some confusion in trying to follow Jones's theories of the backswing. He warned of the danger of arriving at the top of the backswing with too much of the body's weight supported by the left leg, as evidenced by the left heel's not leaving the ground at all in the course of taking the club back for a full shot. "Not only in such a swing is the player prevented from shifting his hips forward as he begins to unwind (on the downswing), but the necessity of maintaining his balance will always force him to fall back upon his right foot

No one is infallible. But when Bobby Jones found the rough, he got out.

as he swings through." In this connection, however, Jones emphasized, as have other authorities on the swing, that the left heel not be deliberately or consciously lifted but rather pulled upward as a consequence of allowing the upper body sufficient freedom to complete a full backswing. The confusion might arise from the fact that Jones also said that in his observation of the best players he had found there was no perceptible shifting of the weight from the left to the right foot during the backstroke. I think the key word here is "perceptible." If, at the position of address, the weight is either equally distributed on both feet or there is a slight preponderance on the left foot (as Jones and others advocated) there must be some shifting to the right side to facilitate the recommended shift to the left side at the start of the downswing. But the backswing weight shift need not necessarily be perceptible, as indeed it probably is not in swingers like Jones who simply turn the body on the backswing with no hint of a lateral movement. There are, however, great players whose backswing weight shift seems to me clearly discernible. I think immediately of Roberto DeVicenzo, who sets up a sort of rocking movement during his swing—a little rock to the right side going back and a more pronounced rock back to the left side on the downward swing. And there was Paul Runyon, who was to me a real "rocker."

I make this point not to dispute Jones—which would be presumptuous indeed—but rather to suggest that maybe he tended to see in others what he himself felt in his own swing. There is this tendency among teachers of golf, however unintentional, and learners of the game have been confused because of it.

Jones was among the first authorities to emphasize that the first and initiating movement of the downswing should be a turning of the hips back around to the left. It was his view that the hips should begin unwinding in this manner even before the backswing is fully completed. Some later authorities expressed the opinion that a correct swing might or might not embody this particular feature. But all have been in agreement that it was certainly desirable, provided it helped the player to avoid leading the downswing with some element other than the hips—the shoulders, for instance, or, worst of all, the hands.

If Jones conceived that the club should follow a significantly different path on the downswing than on the backswing, he made no specific mention of it. Neither, according to my research, did any of the other experts of his day or earlier. It seems apparent that most early authorities figured that the downswing essentially retraced the backswing, or that the point was insufficiently important to warrant particular emphasis. Actually, in stating that the inside-out downswing was a delusion, Jones probably promoted the idea of the backswing and downswing ideally being in the same groove. The more modern theory of the swing—as borne out by the swings of today's best players—holds that the downswing follows an essentially different path from the backswing. (A strong case in point is 1969 Masters champion George Archer.)

In both his swing and his writing, Jones represents a sort of link between past and present as regards a stiffening or straightening of the left leg at the culmination of the downswing. According to published photographs, as well as my own memory, Jones straightened his left leg perceptibly at or near impact. Whether he stiffened it, as advocated by Vardon, would depend on one's personal interpretation of the two terms. I would say that he straightened the left leg as he came into the impact area but did not, in Vardon's phrase, stiffen it "to the point of rigidity." I think that what Jones did was, in the phrase that became and long remained popular, "hit against a firm left side," which is something that few if any top golfers of today do or prescribe.

I think there can be no doubt that Jones took the golfing knowledge of his day, refined it, modified it, and made better use of it than anyone else ever had. Along the way, he added some valuable concepts of his own, and when his playing career was over he passed along what amounted almost to a new body of knowledge about the golf swing. I would not say, as the writers of his day did in their vast enthusiasm for Jones and his exploits, that Jones's swing was "perfect." His swing was, however, one that can be studied with profit, as can the things he said about golf.

Naturally enough, the Jones influence was strongest and most lasting in the Atlanta area. In the years since I first played with Jones and studied his swing, I have played with a

Twenty years after he retired, Jones could still work his magic with the club. Here he is in 1942, when he shot a 145 in the first two rounds in the Hale America Tournament in Atlanta.

number of good players from, in, and around Atlanta. Almost without exception, they had something of the Jones swing in their own swings—the strong position of the left hand on the club, the long, flowing, graceful style, and so on. Even Tommy Aaron, the Georgian who plays so well on today's P.G.A. tour, is reminiscent of Jones in the length and fluidity of his swing, although Tommy is of another generation.

As an example of how the Jones influence became world-wide, I recall that Bobby Locke, the first of the great South African players, told me that to a considerable degree he copied the basics of Jones's swing. And, of course, Locke was in turn the model for most of the good South African players who came after him. Thus did the Jones influence spread to South Africa by way of Great Britain, where the young Locke probably first saw him play.

Ben Hogan

Ben Hogan stands out as the man who had the greatest influence on golf methods and techniques in the era following Bobby Jones. This is not to say that Hogan was, in the tradition of Jones, far and away the best golfer of his time. A vast number of the game's aficionados think he was the best, and they are certainly not lacking for evidence to sustain their position. But Sam Snead and Byron Nelson also have their adherents, and each contributed in his own way to shaping the game's modern concepts.

The question of which of the three was the best golfer is not within the purview of this book. Nor is the question of which had the "best" swing. More to our point is, which of the three holds the strongest position in the succession of great golfers who, like Vardon and Jones, were the dominant influences in the way the game is played today. For the record, however—and because the record does have bearing on the extent of the Hogan influence on the modern golf swing—it should be noted that Hogan won nine major championships, Snead six, and Nelson five. Hogan won the U.S. Open four times, the Masters twice, the P.G.A. twice, and the British Open once. Snead won the Masters three times, the P.G.A. twice, and the British Open once. Nelson won the Masters twice, the P.G.A. twice, and the U.S. Open once. All these are great records, to be sure, but Hogan's clearly stands out. Hogan also stands high in all-time records. He is one of four men in the history of golf to have won all four of these major championships, the others being Gene Sarazen, Gary Player, and Jack Nicklaus. And along with Bobby Jones and Willie Anderson (of the very early era in American golf), he is one of three to have won four U.S. Opens.

There are, I think less tangible but more telling reasons why Hogan's way of playing had and has more of a hold on the imagination of a vast majority of golfers than Snead's or Nelson's—or anybody else's since Jones. For one thing, Hogan had to work much harder and longer to perfect his game than did Snead or Nelson. This fact has strong appeal for other golfers to whom the game did not come naturally, which includes just about all of us. Hogan conveyed the idea that golf could in fact be learned through trial and error plus work and hope, which is the process that just about every aspiring player has to go through.

The records of the three bear this out. Hogan, Snead, and Nelson were born in the same year, 1912; all took up golf at about the same age; and all achieved their first prominence as playing professionals in the late 1930s. Snead began winning pro tournaments right from the start, and it was obvious to all that a superplayer had arrived on the golf scene—there was no mistaking his enormous talent. Even in those earliest days he had what is perhaps the greatest natural swing the game has ever known, and, of course, he never saw much reason to alter it or concern himself about why it worked.

It took Nelson a little longer to bring his game to the championship level. But he was the first of this triumvirate to win a major title, the 1937 Masters. Also in 1937, hardly more than a year after he began his career, Snead was the popular favorite to win the U.S. Open at Oakland Hills in Birmingham, Michigan, and he appeared to have it won until Ralph Guldahl staged a great finish to beat him out. It was the first of Snead's long series of frustrations in the Open, but even in losing he remained the public's choice as the best golfer of that day.

Hogan, meanwhile, was chiefly distinguishing himself for the vast amount of time and effort he spent trying to make himself a winner. He has related that at one time he was running so short of money that he was about to abandon the tour, at least temporarily, while he raised more funds. Anyway, it was to be 1946, at the age of thirty-four, before Hogan won a major championship—the P.G.A. Probably few people realize that despite their great similarity in age and background, Nelson won all of his five major championships before Hogan won the first of his nine. And Nelson announced his retirement as a competitor (except for appearances in the Masters and an occasional tournament elsewhere) before Hogan won his first U.S. Open in 1948.

This late-blooming success is part of the Hogan legend—part of the reason why the public came to admire and respect him so much, both for his skill at the game and his knowledge of it. The apparent line of reasoning is that Hogan worked and thought his way up from a not very good golfer to the greatest in the world, so it was only logical that he would know how a golf swing is transformed from bad to good. In short, those who aspire to greater things in golf—whether it be to break 100 for the first time or win the club championship—tend to feel that they have something in common with Ben Hogan. They see in him reason to keep trying and hoping.

Another important part of the Hogan legend, particularly

The incomparable Hogan swing in his early years.

as it pertains to his reputation for having a very special and perhaps unique knowledge of the mechanics of the golf swing, is that right up through his early and middle fifties he remained, in the estimation of just about every knowledgeable golfer, the finest hitter of the golf ball in the world—past or present. In any golf-oriented conversation, the mere mention of Hogan's name would prompt somebody to say that Hogan could still win any tournament he entered if only he could putt. And this was, if not pure fact, pretty close to it. He could, well over a decade after he won his last major championship in 1953 and was nearing the age of fifty-five, consistently hit shots with amazing power and accuracy. And it is certainly true that in those latter years he was a just plain bad putter, particularly from the 3- to 5-foot range.

(In May of 1967 the editor of this book went on assignment from *Golf Digest* magazine to what has so far turned out to be one of Hogan's last appearances as a competitor—the Colonial National Invitational Open at Fort Worth, Texas. The idea was to watch Hogan play every shot for the full 72 holes and determine, as far as possible, whether he was in fact the best shotmaker in golf from tee to green. Hogan shot 281 for a third-place tie with George Archer. Of the 281 shots, 141 were taken in reaching the greens. Of the 141, 139 were rated from well-executed to superbly executed. The remaining two were a drive that missed the fairway by some 5 yards and a 5-iron to a par-3 hole that missed the green by about the same distance. It was difficult, if not impossible to conceive of anybody hitting the ball better over a four-day span.)

Hogan the golf theorist, as differentiated from Hogan the golf player, first came to the rapt attention of the golf world in 1947. It was then that he made the startling statement that he had discovered the "secret" of hitting a golf ball correctly, and that it would no longer be necessary for him to work so hard at his game or suffer doubts about how his swing would function from day to day. He emphasized that it was indeed a secret, so much so that he would not even reveal it to his wife, let alone to the players against whom he planned to compete for at least several more years.

The statement was especially startling in one respect, as it put Hogan so squarely on the spot. He clearly must have known that he would consistently have to produce some outstanding golf or suffer considerable embarrassment. He surely knew that all serious golfers are prone to come up with what they think "the secret" but which usually turns out to be a snare and a delusion. I know that I have had many of them, some of which I briefly thought were so valuable that I would keep them strictly to myself until I had won all the tournaments and money I wanted to. But none ever impressed me sufficiently or worked for a long enough trial period to tempt me to announce that "now I've really got it." Hogan's did.

On the P.G.A. tour, which I had joined, there was fairly wide speculation about what Hogan's secret might be. There was even more speculation about whether Hogan actually had a secret or whether he was just trying to needle his opponents with a sort of mass injection. In time, many of the pros became inclined to the latter view, or at least had serious doubts. One even went so far as to say that Hogan was "the biggest liar on the tour."

Anyway, during the next six years—or five, if you subtract the year he was out of competition following his near-fatal auto accident—Hogan won eight of his nine major championships. The last of these was his peak year of 1953, when he won the Masters, the U.S. Open, and the British Open.

In 1955, following the first of several years in which the secret produced no major championship, and soon after his great effort to win a fifth U.S. Open was thwarted by Jack Fleck at the Olympic Club in San Francisco, Hogan was prevailed upon by the editors of Life to reveal his secret exclusively in their magazine. The reported inducements included $25,000.

Actually Life had been intrigued by the Hogan secret for

many months. More than a year before Hogan's revelation, *Life* asked a number of Hogan's fellow professionals for their opinion of what it might be. They included Walter Burkemo, Claude Harmon (who had previously said he was privy to the secret), George Fazio (who had been a sort of victim of it when Hogan beat him and Lloyd Mangrum in the playoff for the 1950 U.S. Open), Mike Turnesa, and Gene Sarazen. Only Turnesa and Sarazen came close. They surmised that it had to do with fanning the clubface wide open on the backswing.

As revealed by Hogan, the secret movement did in fact involve a roll or twist of the hands that opens the clubface to a maximum on the backswing. Hogan noted that this facet of the secret was called "pronation" and had been taught by the early Scottish professionals who had come to the United States to teach golf. This pronation, said Hogan, was a vital part of the overall secret but of itself was worth less than nothing without the addition of two specific adjustments. The first of these adjustments, he said, was in the grip—a turn of the left hand about three-eighths of an inch over to the left so that the left thumb lay directly down the top of the shaft and the back of the left hand was just about facing the target. The pronation and the grip adjustment, he went on to explain, set things up for the second adjustment, which was the "real meat" of the secret.

I cupped the (left) wrist gradually backward and inward on the backswing so that the wrist formed a slight V at the top of the swing. The angle was not more than four or six degrees, almost invisible to the human eye. This simple maneuver, in addition to the pronation, had the effect of opening the face of the club to the widest practical extreme at the top of the swing.

At this point the swing had been made hook-proof. No matter how hard I swung or how hard I tried to roll into and through the ball, the face of the clubhead could not close fast enough to become absolutely square at the moment of impact. The result was that lovely, long-fading ball which is a highly effective weapon on any golf course.

In essence, Hogan was saying that if you open the club-face to the "widest practical extreme" on the backswing, it becomes physically impossible to close it enough on the downswing to make the ball hook. This naturally raises the question of what the player does when he wants to hook—the hook being at times a highly effective weapon on any golf course. Hogan said he produced the hook simply by eliminating the wrist-cupping feature. From all of which, it would seem to follow logically that he would produce a straight ball by partially eliminating the wrist-cupping feature—creating a slightly more shallow V at the top of the backswing of, say, two to three degrees.

For the average golfer, this explanation would seem to be so highly theoretical and intricate as to be of value only insofar as it provides an insight into how an extremely fine golfer swung the club during one phase of a brilliant career. Hogan himself, surely to the disappointment of a great many readers of Life, said near the end of the article, "I doubt that it will be worth a doggone to the weekend duffer and it will ruin a bad golfer." In an earlier Life article, Sarazen, who had surmised that the secret was "pronation," went even further: "It would wreck the game of anybody else who used it," he pronounced.

(Most interesting to me from a personal standpoint, Hogan said in concluding the Life article, "Now that I am through with serious competition . . . I don't mind letting the world in on my secret. . . . I hope it helps some distinguished but frustrated golfer get to next year's U.S. Open at Rochester, New York, who might not have got there otherwise. I expect to be there to see if anything new has been added." Hogan was there, all right, and I got the definite impression that he was competing seriously. I won that Open (1956). Hogan finished one stroke out, the vital difference being a missed 3-foot putt by Hogan at the 71st hole.)

By Hogan's estimate, a bare 10 percent of all golfers possess a sufficiently high degree of skill to use the principles of his secret to their advantage. By my estimate, that would probably include players with established handicaps of not more than 6. For golfers who feel ready to use it, or hope to become so, some background knowledge of how and where Hogan worked it out will be especially helpful. For other golfers, the information should be of general interest and helpful in understanding the mechanics of golf swings.

As indicated earlier, Hogan was looking for a way to keep from hooking the ball, or at least to minimize and control his natural hook. Along with such other notable golfers as the late Lawson Little, Hogan was firmly of the opinion that a correctly executed golf swing, lacking any compensating or offsetting movements, naturally and automatically produced a hook. The implication is that to hit a straight ball or a fade, the good natural swinger must go against his instincts and somehow modify his swing. "The mechanics of a good swing demands a hook," said Hogan back in 1955. There is presumptive evidence that Hogan later changed some of his theories, or at least modified them, but what he theorized in and before 1955 is important to an understanding of the theories generally held today.

As a hooker, Hogan made most of his errors to the left side of the target, as hookers are wont to do. And, as is also characteristic of players who habitually hook, the errors he made to the right of the target came through aiming too far to the right in anticipation of the hook and getting less of it than expected. A good golfer can, of course, also fight a hook by deliberately trying to slice or fade the ball, but this is generally an unreliable weapon. It is what is called trying to correct a fault with a fault, and even when it works insofar as accuracy is concerned, it does so at the cost of a considerable loss in distance. So the constant enemy remains the hook, accountable for errors both left and right or loss of valuable distance.

What Hogan was looking for, then, was a method that would eliminate the hook except when needed and at the same time cause no appreciable loss of distance. He said he found it in the secret after leaving the tour and going home to Fort Worth to meditate on the golf swing for three or four days—or however long it might take to find an answer—during which time he didn't pick up a golf club. He was desperate about the current state and probable future of his golf game, he said, and he surely must have been because that was no doubt the longest period in his life since age twelve that he had gone without picking up a golf club, except perhaps during his service in World War II.

Hogan, it should be noted, was ideally equipped to work out a highly technical and involved golf problem in his mind. As he once said, he had for most of his life devoted all of his waking hours and some of his sleeping ones to the theory and practice of golf. There was surely no theory adduced up to that time that he had not considered and tested at one time or another, singly and in various combinations. It is easy to picture him during those troubled three or four days like some scientist abandoning his laboratory and trying to think on a higher plane than before—saying to himself that perhaps there must be some element or combination of elements that he had somehow overlooked. And then, so to speak, this apple plopped right down on his head. As has happened in many discoveries, he took an old principle generally thought to be outmoded (pronation) and added a couple of refinements of his own (the grip alteration and the wrist-cupping business).

In his instructional writing, Hogan made no mention of the pronation and wrist-cupping maneuver on the backswing. To the contrary, he stated that the clubface should remain square to the ball throughout the backswing instead of being opened to the widest practical angle. His last book, *The Modern Fundamentals of Golf*, was published in 1957, and as recently as 1969 he stated that it embodied all his basic theories of the golf swing, although he had continued to experiment in the hope that he could add something new to the theory of the game.

Hogan made it clear that he considered some of his ideas to be revolutionary, which is to say that he considered the early authorities to be wrong on certain points. "As I see it," said Hogan, "some measures long esteemed to be of paramount importance in the golf swing are not important at all. On the other hand, certain other measures that have been considered to be of only secondary importance (or of no importance at all) strike me as being invaluable—to be, in fact, the true fundamentals of the modern golf swing."

In the vital matter of the grip, Hogan did not greatly differ with such early and eminent authorities as Vardon or Jones as to the placement of the hands on the club. He did advocate turning the left hand more around to the left than did either Vardon or Jones, but this would represent more of an adjustment or modification than a basic difference. Where earlier authorities had said that the V's formed by the thumb and index finger of each hand should form a straight line pointing to the right shoulder, Hogan said that the V of the left hand should point to the right eye and the right-hand V to the chin. The average golfer might consider these differences negligible, but the expert is keenly aware that his grip must be correct in even the smallest detail and that it must not vary from one swing to the next.

On the matter of relative finger pressure in the grip, Hogan in effect completely reversed the Vardon theory of maximum pressure applied by the thumb and index finger of each hand. With the left hand, said Hogan, the main pressure should be in the last three fingers. With the right hand, the thumb and index finger should rest on the club as lightly as possible. He suggested a practice-swing exercise with these two fingers completely off the club. As with all the points he made about the golf swing, Hogan had a precise explanation. He said that pressure in the thumb and first finger activated muscles along the outside of the forearm, and that these were not the muscles to be used in the golf swing.

One of the previously little-esteemed measures that Hogan regarded as being of prime importance is standing to the ball with the right foot pointing straight ahead at an exact right angle with the intended line of flight, and the left foot a quarter of a turn outward—a quarter, that is, of 90 degrees, or about 22 degrees, to be more precise. This squared position of the right foot at address is a key to Hogan's overall theory of the golf swing and is indicative of a departure from other long-held theories, notably that the hips should take a full, free turn on the backswing. Bobby Jones, among other pre-Hogan theorists, stressed the desirability of the full hip-turn, and at least one notable golf writer said that the big hip-turn was the "secret" of Jones's success. Hogan, far from advocating a full hip-turn on the backswing, said that a part of the central idea was to retard the turning of the hips going back, at least to an extent sufficient to insure that the hips turned considerably less than the shoulders did. In this connection, Hogan said that it was impossible to turn the shoulders too far around, provided the head remained in place. He specified that the shoulders should turn enough to put the player's back to the target, and he noted that Sam Snead was especially fortunate in that he was supple enough to turn his shoulders past this point so that his back was facing several degrees to the right of the target. So, too, as I recall, was Bobby Jones.

The right foot turned outward, as virtually all early authorities advocated it should be, gives freer play to a backward turn of the hips but has little if any effect on the degree to which the shoulders turn. The squared right foot retards the turning of the hips while not appreciably affecting the shoulder turn. As Hogan put it, the right foot pointing straight ahead "acts as a governor" to permit the hips to turn to the extent that they should and no more.

In all this, Hogan was making the point that there should

be a stretching and tightening of the muscles that control the movement of the hips. With these muscles thus stretched and made taut as a result of the retarded hip-turn and the full shoulder-turn, the body becomes properly coiled so that it is a natural and automatic thing for the player to lead the downswing with a turning of the hips back around to the left—the true key to setting in motion the power-generating elements of the swing in the correct order.

Other theorists had, of course, stressed that the hips should lead the downswing but did not, as Hogan did, tie this movement to a certain positioning of the right foot at address. Others merely said that the hips should lead the downswing. Hogan did not dispute that the downswing could be correctly initiated even though a full turn of the hips was taken, but he noted that the player would then have to make the movement on his own rather than have it come about automatically. "If you permit the hips to turn too much on the backswing, this tension and torsion are lost and there's nothing to start them forward."

In advocating that the left foot should be turned outward, Hogan was adding nothing new. That goes at least back to Vardon, and it has always been generally agreed that this positioning of the left foot facilitates the downswing movement of the hips and makes it easier for the player to move freely into and through the ball.

Of all golf theorists, Hogan placed by far the most importance on the waggle—the series of movements that come between taking the stance and starting the backswing. Jones and Vardon, for instance, gave the waggle little more than passing mention, indicating that one rather casual loosening-up movement of the clubhead with the hands was normally sufficient. Hogan called the waggle an integral part of the swing and described precisely how it should be carried out. He noted that he first became aware of the importance of the waggle in 1932, chiefly by noting how Johnny Revolta used it to advantage in gearing his swing for short shots, from which premise Hogan reasoned that it would be helpful on full shots as well.

As to the movements involved in the waggle, back away from the ball, Hogan said that with the left hand in control, the lower part of the arm should be rotated slightly, the right elbow should hit the front part of the right hip, and the left elbow should come out slightly. On the forward waggle, he said, the left hand also moves an inch or two past the ball toward the target.

As precise as he was about the movements of the waggle, Hogan placed greater stress on the rhythm, which he said should be geared to the type of shot planned—slow and soft for a soft high shot; faster and brisker for a low shot to be drilled into the wind, and so on, always making the waggle a rehearsal procedure for the shot to come. Among current players, Gardner Dickinson carries out the waggle very nearly as Hogan prescribed. In contrast, Doug Sanders exhibits the technique of virtually no waggle at all.

Concerning the backswing itself, Hogan departed from earlier concepts not so much in the way he carried it out as in the way he conceived it and in the phases of it he chose to stress. He said it should be started simply by extending the arc of the waggle by adding to the waggle a turn of the shoulders, which during the waggle itself do not move. As we have seen, the order of backswing movement prescribed by Hogan is hands, arms, shoulders, hips. This in general reverses the order advocated by earlier theorists but is scarcely a point on which the learning golfer should dwell, since the movements should be, for all practical purposes, almost simultaneous.

Hogan moves farthest away from other theorists in the relative stress he places on swinging the club back in the correct plane. This clearly is one of the points he had in mind when he made his statement that "some measures long esteemed to be of paramount importance . . . are really not important at all". . . and "certain other measures that have been considered to be of only secondary importance (or of no importance at all) strike me as being invaluable. . . ." He obviously placed the arc of the backswing in the first category and the plane in the second. As to the arc, he said it was regulated by keeping the left arm fully extended—therefore it sort of took care of itself. But he felt the plane to be a different, and far more vital, matter.

To establish the correct plane, the player sees that his stance and posture are basically correct—feet about as far apart as the width of the shoulders, knees flexed, back generally straight. Then he imagines a straight line running from the level of his shoulders downward and outward to the ball. The player should swing the club back on this exact plane, or, failing that, slightly below it—never above it.

The matter of the plane, the importance of which Hogan says he first grasped in 1938, largely disposes of the old question of how flat or upright the swing should be. As Hogan puts it, a tall player with relatively short arms will appear to have an upright swing if he stays on his correct plane, while a player of short stature will, with the same stipulation, appear to have a flat swing. But, in Hogan's firm opinion at least, if they are good swingers they will be neither flat nor upright, in the generally accepted sense of these terms, but on the same relative plane. Hogan himself appeared to have a flatter swing than most good players, while much taller players, such as Al Geiberger and Tom Weiskopf, appear to swing quite upright.

Hogan's view of the correct downswing is that it proceeds almost automatically from what has gone before, provided only that it is initiated by a turning of the left hip back around to the left. He notes that the action following the start of the downswing takes place so swiftly that the player has by then, in Hogan's phrase, become the captive of a good swing or a bad one, depending on his prior technique.

As to the time-honored axiom of keeping the eye on the ball and not raising the head, he said these things come naturally in a good swing, and the opposite (looking up) comes equally naturally and can't be avoided in a bad swing. Thus he throws out looking up as the cause of a bad swing and instead labels it the result. (The same line of reasoning, of course, applies to the follow-through. In discussing the follow-through, Hogan repudiates the old Vardon theory about the stiffening of the left leg as the ball is hit and the clubhead moves through. Hogan firmly states that the knees are flexed to the same degree at the finish of the swing as at the start, and that in fact the degree of flex should not change during any stage of the swing. He stresses that the hips should keep turning back around to the left until the player's mid-section faces a point several degrees to the left of the target, which would not be physically possible if the left leg stiffened at impact.

Hogan also at least partially repudiates a number of long-held theories about what the hands do, or should do, during the downswing—particularly those theories that hold that the hit is delivered principally with one hand or the other. He states that hitting the ball correctly is a joint action of the two hands. He also made this startling (to some) statement about the hands: "The main thing for the novice or the average golfer is to keep any conscious hand action out of the swing. The correct swing is founded on chain action, and if you use the hands when you shouldn't, you prevent this chain action.

Some earlier theorists who set down their views on the golf swing, notably Walter J. Travis and Seymour Dunn, conceived of the overall golf swing as following a circular path, with the downswing retracing that part of the circle first traced by the backswing. Travis, the fine American turn-of-the-century amateur, said that every golf swing should form some part of a circle." Dunn, who was chiefly noted as a teacher rather than a player, used compass drawings to emphasize his point about the circular character of the swing. Hogan, although by no means the first to depart from the circle theory (back and down in the same groove), was among the first to emphasize that the downswing should follow an essentially different path from the backswing. "The plane for the downswing is less steeply inclined and is oriented with the ball quite differently from the backswing plane." In his repudiation of Bobby Jones's strong statement that trying to hit the ball from the inside out was nonsense, Hogan said that to generate maximum power the player must hit from the inside out.

In his description of the correct downswing path, Hogan noted that the vital movement of turning the hips to start the downswing necessarily and automatically dropped the hands to about the level of the hips along a considerably more steeply inclined path than the hands properly follow on the backswing. Thus the sharp descent of the hands to hip level positions them and the clubhead in such a way that the rest of the downswing must follow a path quite different from the comparable segment of the backswing. As noted, the downswing moves far too fast for its path to be regulated by conscious effort, but knowing in advance what the path should be adds to the player's understanding of the swing, thereby helping him to be a better swinger.

In essence, Hogan conceived the downswing as a chain reaction in which each power-generating element after the first multiplied the force created by the preceding one. As in any chain reaction, the elements must be set off in the prescribed order or the whole thing will fizzle out; the prescribed order being hips, shoulders, arms, hands. The steps leading up to the firing-off of the first stage (the start of the downswing) also must be correctly carried out to insure the success of the operation.

When Hogan put together his theories in book form in 1957, he was confident that they could serve to make any conscientious student of them consistently break 80. Ten years later, as he reached the end of his brilliant competitive career, he wasn't sure of just how much they would help the average player, although he had no doubts about their being right. "My way of hitting the ball is right for me," he said. Then he added, somewhat ruefully, "I really don't know if they are right for everybody else." But on his record as a player, and apart from the long and intense study he gave to the game, his theories are clearly worthy of study.

My own experience with Hogan and his golf game (it is hard to think of them separately) began in the since-discontinued North-South Open at Pinehurst, North Carolina, in 1945, and extended for more than twenty years, during all of which I never ceased to be impressed with his ability to hit golf shots (as goes without saying) and his capacity for analyzing the swing. In the latter connection, it was Ben who first told me and explained to me that it was impossible to commit the fatal error of starting the downswing with the hands (hitting from the top) if you moved the body correctly—about as valuable a lesson as a golfer can learn.

We were, of course, paired together in tournaments many, many times. Also, we were frequent playing companions both in practice rounds for upcoming tournaments and simply for the sake of playing. We talked golf a lot, on and off the course. He rarely volunteered to expound on his theories, but if you asked him a valid question, he would willingly give you a clear answer. And I asked him many questions.

To me the most memorable example of Hogan's ability to analyze the swing came just before the U.S. Open in 1955 at the Olympic Club at San Francisco. A full week before the tournament started, we played a practice round at Olympic, which is a course that demands the frequent use of a controlled hook. Using the fade, to which he had by then habituated himself, Hogan played badly. "I'll see you boys in three or four days," he told us at the end of the round. He took his clubs and practice balls and left. We knew he was on his way to some golf course in the area where, in relative privacy, he could develop the kind of a hook that would fit the Olympic golf course. He came back with it in the stipulated three or four days, and it is a familiar story how, within the next few days, he came closer than had any other golfer to winning a fifth U.S. Open.

Going back to the North-South Open of 1945, which I won as an amateur and in which I played the last 36 holes with Hogan, I remember that he had what struck me as an exceptionally long backswing, dropping the club well below the horizontal at the end of it. In 1947, when I joined the P.G.A. tour and began to see him regularly, I noticed that he had shortened his backswing some. I later learned that he had accomplished this shortening by going from what is known as the long thumb to the short thumb—meaning that instead of extending the left thumb far down the shaft, which facilitates a longer backswing, he was placing the left thumb so that it covered about half-an-inch less of the shaft. (I also was to learn considerably later that Hogan said he first came to have real confidence in his game in 1946, which took a slight—but only slight—edge off my having beaten him in the North-South a year earlier.)

By 1948 it was obvious that Hogan opened the clubface and began his wrist-cocking (cupping) early in the backswing. And he almost invariably made the ball move from left to right on full shots. Most were slight fades, with the ball moving gradually to the right, but on some shots—drives in particular—he would actually slice the ball. But the main thing I and his other fellow pros noticed was that he almost invariably put the ball just about where he wanted to.

After Hogan came back on the tour early in 1950—having been off it for almost a year because of the highway accident —he mostly hit the ball straight instead of fading it. But if he hit one hook, he would go back to the fade for the rest of the round, unless, of course, he needed a deliberate hook. Also in this early post-accident period, he would sometimes use a fairway wood for a shot of 215 yards or so, a distance from which he would normally use a 2-iron. On these shots he would fade the ball rather sharply by hitting down on it and across it, leaving a divot-mark that pointed well to the left of the target.

He always seemed to have all the shots that the rest of us did, plus a few in reserve.

My impression is that in the later years he made considerably less use of the so-called secret that gave him a guaranteed left-to-right movement of the ball in flight. Sometimes, as when he would come to a relatively short par-4 hole with a very narrow fairway, he would take his driver and hit what some of us called "a dinky little ol' slice." Esthetically, so to speak, the shot didn't look like much, but it always seemed to wind up either in the center of the fairway or on whichever portion of the fairway that offered the best second-shot position.

Certainly there is no reason to believe that Hogan hit on one particular swing technique in 1947 or thereabouts and used it for virtually all shots from then on. He never stopped experimenting, and he never stopped learning. He could not otherwise have been the consummate master of the game that he was for a good twenty years.

Hogan has retired as a tournament competitor, but he may return to play in an occasional tournament. His influence on modern golf swings and techniques, however, will remain strong. I think it is a fair statement to make that every playing professional who was contemporary with Hogan for any length of time studied him in action and learned something from him. There always seemed to be at least a few around whenever he was practicing. It often happened that a player who was hitting out balls himself would stop to watch when Hogan arrived on the practice tee. The inference is that they figured they could improve themselves more by studying Hogan than by practicing their own techniques.

Sam Snead
—Doin' What Comes
Naturally

In the most recent treatise on golf that bears
his name (*Sam Snead on Golf*) Snead's opening line is,
"Playing golf is like eating; it's something which has to come
naturally." Another instructional book by Snead bore the
title of *Natural Golf*.

Golf did in fact come easily and naturally to Snead. When
he first came on the P.G.A. tour in 1936, he had the same
fluid, graceful, seemingly effortless swing that was to remain
with him for more than thirty years—and which, even after
that time, gave no sign of change. He never tried to probe
deeply into the mechanics of the swing, because he never felt
any need to. Hogan once said to me that "Sam don't know
a damn thing about hitting a golf ball, but he does it better
than anybody else." Another time, in a panel discussion of the
golf swing and how best to present the theory of it in print,

Paul Runyon derided Snead's comments on the grounds that Snead had so much natural ability that he couldn't possibly have any insight into the problems that beset other golfers. As for myself, I think Snead had a good understanding of his own swing, but I doubt that he ever concerned himself greatly about the subtleties of the game as they relate to other and lesser players. It is not his basic nature to think along these lines, although he gave many lessons and was considered a good teacher.

Nevertheless, Snead did make at least one valuable contribution to the presently held theories of the game: He gave golfers a fuller and better concept of swing tempo.

Theorists in the early days of golf paid scant attention to tempo (or timing), except to say that the backswing should be slow and that the downswing should not be hurried from the top. This naturally raises the question of just how slow the backswing should be, and what characterizes a downswing that is too hurried from the top. Nowadays it is understood that the business of the slow backswing can easily be overdone, to the detriment of the overall swing and that the downswing should be as fast as possible, provided acceleration is gradual and that its power-generating elements are brought to bear in the correct sequence. What it comes to is that a good golf swing has tempo, rhythm, timing—apply whichever term you prefer—and Snead exemplifies this principle as perhaps no other golfer has. If you were trying to explain correct swing tempo to a beginning player, the clearest way to do it would be to cite the example of Snead. Many touring professionals liked to be paired with Snead because they could subconsciously absorb his great sense of tempo by watching him swing. This is not to say that every golfer should try to have the same swing tempo that Snead does. Snead's is an ideal tempo, but it would not necessarily suit every golfer. If you pay particular attention to Snead, you are bound to notice that the tempo of his golf swing is in accord with the way he walks and does things other than hit a golf ball—all litheness and grace, neither fast nor slow.

There is a saying in golf that the ideal opponent is a man with a fast backswing and a fat pocketbook. There is an element of truth in the saying, but it needs to be qualified. To cite an outstanding example, there is the amateur Billy Joe Patton, whose overall swing is so fast that the clubhead is a blur from the time he starts his backswing until he completes his follow-through. Arnold Palmer also takes the club back briskly and certainly qualifies in the fat-pocketbook category, as does Patton. Yet both men would be more apt to invade your pocketbook than you would theirs. At the other end of the scale, there is amateur Harvie Ward, who is very leisurely going back and starts the clubhead down so slowly that you can almost literally read the name of the manufacturer on the top of it until he reaches the impact segment of the swing. All these players have good tempo. But the point about Snead is that he so clearly shows what good tempo is and how it serves to make a golf swing functional.

As exemplified by all good golfers, and so outstandingly by Snead, setting the correct tempo begins even before the player takes his stance. He should be gearing himself to the desired tempo as he approaches the ball preparatory to taking his stance. He should be thinking rhythm and smoothness and guarding against being hurried or jerky in any phase of the swing, from waggle to follow-through. As a matter of fact, the good golfer thinks of tempo from the moment he steps on the first tee until he completes the round, which is to say that he tries to maintain an even pace at all times. The unthinking golfer will—especially when the pressure of a close match is mounting or the shot coming up is particularly tough—begin to take on a hurried and harried manner as he walks between shots, which will naturally carry over into the swing he takes when he gets to the ball.

The objective of good tempo is to insure that the downswing is started smoothly with the hips leading and the rest of the power-generating elements following smoothly in their proper sequence. Everything that goes before the transition from backswing to downswing has that objective. I think that any golfer who gives the matter thought will recognize that hurried and jerky movements leading up to the start of the downswing will produce a downswing start of like character. To fix the point clearly in mind, he can find a prime example of what is correct by watching Snead.

A discerning student of the swing will notice that Snead's swing tempo is a bit slower than Hogan's. The close observer also will note that Snead departs slightly from the Hogan theory of the placement of the feet at address. Snead turns his right foot slightly outward, facilitating a fuller and freer turn of the hips on the backswing. But then, Snead takes a bigger

GOLF DIGEST

Sam Snead's patented smooth swing through the impact area, shown here and on the following two pages.

turn of the shoulders than Hogan—and nearly all other golfers—so he has no real need to retard the turning of the hips going back. He still gets the proper body coil by turning the shoulders more than the hips, which is the central idea.

It seems characteristic of Snead, with his emphasis on swinging naturally, to advise learning golfers simply and straightforwardly to "hit the ball straight." It would be unlike him to laboriously work out a method of hitting a fade, as Hogan did. Actually, Snead has always instinctively been something of a hooker, bearing out the theory that a good natural swing tends to produce a hook. Snead's rare bad shots

were hooks a bit out of control or misses to the right, normally brought on by overcompensating for his hook.

As to the grip, Snead went along more with Bobby Jones than with Hogan. He advised that the V's formed by the thumb and index finger of each hand should form a straight line pointing to the right shoulder. Most strictly modern theorists—excepting Billy Casper, who uses the strong positioning of the left hand—would label this grip out of date. But it was Snead's natural grip from the beginning, so naturally he kept it.

Byron Nelson

It seems logical to assume that Byron Nelson
had and will have a lesser influence on the modern golf swing
than either of his great contemporaries and long-time rivals,
Hogan and Snead. It is a situation dictated by history and cir-
cumstance. Nelson's peak playing years having coincided
with World War II, his marvelous skills did not get the attention they would have gotten in a later time. And perhaps as
importantly in the matter of influence, Nelson's retirement as
a full-time competitor came just before televised golf became
popular. Thus Nelson was seen in person by only a few of
the golfers who would come to prominence after World
War II, and did not become a familiar figure on television
screens as did Hogan and Snead.

Nelson wrote some valuable instructional material around
the time of his retirement, but in later years he chose to impart his vast and intimate knowledge of the golf swing only to

The instant of impact—Byron Nelson's swing that won him eleven straight tournaments in eighteen victories during one season.

a few exceptionally talented players through individual instruction. These included Ken Venturi, who was very much in the forefront of the golf scene for a number of years (and could be again if a cure is found for a hand ailment that has largely kept him out of the game in recent years), and Marty Fleckman, one of the rising young stars. Much of the Nelson technique can be seen in Venturi and Fleckman.

I have played with Nelson many times, even though he essentially retired from the P.G.A. tour the same year I joined it (1947). In my view, he was simply an extremely sound swinger with two or three particularly distinctive movements that set his swing apart from that of Hogan or Snead. I would say that Nelson perfected the technique of cocking the wrists after starting the downswing instead of at the top of the backswing. This was his way of insuring against hitting from the top. Also, he had an exceptionally strong lateral movement of the lower part of the body on the downswing. The knees as well as the hips moved strongly in the direction of the target. Oddly, among the modern-era players, it is Gardner Dickinson who most resembles Nelson in the downswing movement of the lower part of the body, although Dickinson is known as a disciple and protégé of Hogan. Additionally, Nelson had a slight but discernible lateral movement of the upper part of the body on the backswing—what some purists might characterize as a sway. This latter movement can be seen in the swing of Frank Beard, one of the most successful of the current P.G.A. tour players. The point seems to be that a slight lateral movement away from the ball on the backswing is no handicap, provided the golfer reacts to it and recovers at the right stage of the downswing.

Whatever his methods, Nelson hit the ball amazingly straight. In their primes, Hogan brought the ball into the target from left to right, Snead from right to left, and Nelson on a dead-straight line. He could, of course, fade the ball or turn it from right to left, and he fairly often did one or the other on his drives. He was a master at using the contour of the fairway to get himself extra length on his tee shots. If a drive down the right side of the fairway with a little draw on it would catch a downhill slope and get extra roll, for example, that's what Nelson would hit. He didn't pioneer this strategic technique, but he raised it to new heights and popularized it among the golfers then and now who have the accuracy and confidence to use it.

As happens with virtually all golfers who achieve a lofty position in the game, Nelson set down his theories of the game in writing, in 1946, very near the end of his career as a full-time competitor. He said that he found writing about golf considerably harder than playing the game, implying that in his playing days he had given little thought to the techniques best-suited to golfers in the bulk. Nelson worked very hard to perfect the methods best-suited to Nelson and, having found them, dedicated himself for the next decade or so to using them to win championships. It was sometime later that he turned his mind to the theoretical aspects of the swing—to considering the various parts rather than the whole.

Nelson definitely favored what we have described as the strong grip—which, in strictly modern terms, would be called a hook grip. It is logical to assume that it would have been a hook grip for Nelson, too, except for the compensating factors of the delayed wrist cock (and uncock) and the very strong lateral thrust of the lower body on the downswing. As to the former, Nelson said, "At no time (on the backswing) make a conscious effort to cock the wrists. . . . It is the deliberate attempt to do so that causes looseness in your swing—and this is a severe detriment to accuracy and consistency." He makes no particular point in the text of the strong sidewise thrust extending from the hips through the knees, but the sequence photographs of his downswing amply convey the message.

As to the stance, Nelson held firmly to the then-prevalent theory that both feet should be turned outward. He saw no need to square the right foot. He also favored a closed stance for the woods, a square stance for the longer irons, and an open stance for the shorter irons.

He said of the start of the backswing:

> *The clubhead is kept low as it starts back from the ball by the shifting of weight laterally from the left foot to the right foot. This lateral motion is important. A grave and common error in starting the backswing is a turning motion with the hips, which causes the club to cut too sharply inside as it is drawn away from the ball.*

Here we have Nelson himself saying in effect that he did in fact have a bit of a lateral movement of the body as he took the club back, and that he considered this motion an integral part of his swing. He makes no apology for this advocacy of what has been held to be a fault by so many other experts— those who have strongly insisted that there should be no hint of a lateral move of the body on the backswing but only a turn of the body on a fixed axis.

The Nelson "sway," to give it the term generally used by its detractors, was very slight, as is the similar move that Frank Beard deliberately incorporates in his own swing. A stronger and more readily apparent move of the same character was used by Hillman Robbins, Jr., of Memphis, the National Amateur champion of 1957 and one of the half-dozen best amateur players through the 1950s. Robbins, incidentally, felt that Nelson was the best golfer in the history of the game. Yet, to the severe detriment of his accuracy and consistency, Robbins kept trying to eliminate this lateral backswing movement. He was continually urged to do so by a couple of purist-theorists who reasoned—quite wrongly as it turned out—that if he could play that well with a sway he could play even better without it.

Few players ever moved their hips as strongly as Nelson did at the start of the downswing, but he described his backswing start in different terms. "My first (downswing) move is the beginning of transfer of weight back from my right to my left side. I am conscious of pulling the club down with the left hip and shoulder. This leaves my hands ready to do their work as the clubhead enters the hitting zone."

As to what he sensed himself doing in the hitting zone, Nelson said:

> I have the sensation of my right hand trying to catch up with my left. This is the release of power that gives your clubhead speed. The only way to get maximum clubhead speed is through unleashing the full power of your hands as the clubhead enters the hitting area—the last 20 inches before clubhead impact with ball.

Nelson said that the left hand should not roll over at any point during the swing.

> The back of the left hand is toward your objective all the time your hands are taking the clubhead into the hitting area, and on through the early stages of the follow-through. This method increases accuracy and consistency. It is a sure cure for the common and disastrous fault of rolling your wrists (turning the left under and the right over, as the clubhead progresses into the follow-through stage of the swing).

Science and Hogan

Recently, a team of distinguished British scientists, working with top British and American golfers, made an in-depth study of the physical principles involved in hitting a golf ball. The research took some five years and the findings were published in a book entitled *The Search for the Perfect Golf Swing*. In the conduct of the search, they devised a "model" to represent a golf swing as nearly perfect as a human being—within the physical limitations of the human anatomy —could make it. Not surprisingly, the swing that most nearly measured up to the model's representation of perfection belonged to Ben Hogan. "Near perfection," they called Hogan's swing. The "perfect" features found in the Hogan swing included a one-piece takeaway; no attempt made to hold the clubface square to the clubface arc; the sequence of maintained tension in the downswing with the legs, hips, torso, shoulders, arms, and wrists acting in that order, and no "slack" being allowed to develop; the turn and sidewise thrust of the hips starting the downswing and setting the whole upper structure in motion as one unit with little or no relative movement of the shoulders and club; the fixed pivot throughout the downswing; the 90-degree roll of the left forearm into impact accomplished while the hands travel a relatively short distance; and the slightly arched left wrists at impact.

Also not surprisingly, the scientists were in almost complete agreement with the golf-swing theories Hogan had expressed less scientifically several years earlier. In sum, they placed Hogan at the top of their list both in performance and theoretical knowledge. They even agreed in effect with the misgivings implied in Hogan's recent statement that his methods might not necessarily work for all other golfers. Science found the squared right foot at address a basically good thing, provided it is reasonably natural for the player to stand to the ball that way. But for a pigeon-toed person, or one whose feet are naturally turned outward in walking or standing, the unnaturalness of taking his stance with the toe of the right foot pointing straight would constitute a handicap. This, incidentally, is a point on which I have always been in mild disagreement with Hogan, partly because whenever the matter comes up I recall an excellent amateur—Jimmy Wittenberg of Memphis—whose toes naturally turn inward and who gets best results by standing to the ball that way.

It appears that the Hogan "secret" is scientifically sound and that, as Hogan surmised, it can be used to advantage by about one player in ten. If you roll the clubhead open by some 120 degrees (which is about the maximum possible, with 90 degrees being approximately normal), then you have to roll it back very quickly on the downswing to get it square, or nearly so, at impact. This type of backswing makes it easier to keep the right elbow tucked in close to the body, for one thing, and makes for freer action in building up clubhead speed on the downswing, but it also places extra importance on timing and takes quite a good player to carry out the action correctly with a reasonable degree of consistency.

Hogan's concept of the backswing plane fits in exactly with the findings of science. He was not necessarily ahead of his time in the use of the concept—the great players who preceded him, took the club back in a basically correct plane—but he was first to define and describe it precisely and to establish its importance.

Hogan was particularly dogmatic about the grip. To him there was only one correct grip, which he had found after years of experimentation, and he was sure that any variant of it was essentially incorrect. "In golf," he said, "there are certain things that you must do quite precisely, where being approximately right is not enough. The grip is one of those areas. . . ." In the scientific view, there is a grip that is right for every player as an individual, and it would necessarily embody most of the basic principles laid down by Hogan, but it could permissibly vary in certain details. One person's hands and, in particular, his wrists, can and do vary in construction from another's, and the grip best-suited to each of them would figure to vary at least slightly. The same line of reasoning, of course, carries over into the swing, as regards specific minor details.

Hogan was a few years ahead of science and his fellow golf theorists in stating that the powerful muscles around the hips and upper thighs are major sources of power in hitting a golf ball. Here again, others may have sensed that fact without stating it directly. In any event, the scientific search for the extra power that distinguishes the extremely long hitter like Tom Weiskopf and Jack Nicklaus found it to be in the exceptional strength or more efficient use of these muscles. Hogan, in his mid-fifties, could still drive with fine players half his age or less.

Hogan may have been righter than he realized when he said that a player becomes a captive of his swing once the downswing is initiated. Tests revealed that once launched into the first stage of his downswing, the player could do nothing to alter its course. The lapsed time between the start of the downswing and the meeting of clubhead and ball is a fourth to a fifth of a second. Coincidentally, this is very close to the least amount of time it takes for the brain to receive and act on a signal from elsewhere in the body. Hence, the brain could get a signal that something had gone wrong and order a correction during the backswing, or possibly at the very start of the downswing. But after that it would be too late. Hogan may not have known much about reaction times in fractions of a second, but with what he knew about golf he didn't have to.

Tommy Armour
Player-Teacher

In the related fields of playing golf and teaching it, very few men have achieved worldwide fame in both. One who did was the late Tommy Armour. Armour won the United States Open in 1927, the Western Open in 1929, the P.G.A. in 1930, and the British Open in 1931. This is a record of major championships that only a handful of players can match, and it takes on added luster in the light of the fact that it was compiled against such opposition as Walter Hagen and Gene Sarazen and, in the U.S. Open, Bobby Jones. In his peak years, Armour was generally conceded to be the finest iron-shot player in the game.

In later years he attained equal fame as a teacher. Aspiring golfers came literally from all over the world to learn from him, and he commanded the highest lesson fees ever paid. These high fees, plus the fact that he taught only at highly

Tommy Armour, one of golf's finest players and teachers.

exclusive places, necessarily limited his clientele, with the result that only a few thousand golfers came under his personal influence. But in 1953 he finally consented to set down his theories in writing, which greatly expanded his influence. With the publication of his book, *How To Play Your Best Golf All the Time*, students of the game figured they could get for a few dollars what Armour's regular pupils paid hundreds of dollars for. The book reportedly sold more copies than any other in the field of golf instruction.

Armour harbored no doubts that his theories were the correct ones, and he presented them positively and convincingly, both to his in-person pupils and his readers. As to the grip, Armour was in virtually all respects in line with the theories generally held during his peak playing years. He favored the strong position of the left hand, with the V formed by the thumb and forefinger pointing to the right shoulder and the first three knuckles visible when looking straight down from the position of address. He held that the key to a correct grip was that the little finger of the left hand should retain a firm hold on the club under the strain put on it at the top of the backswing. The left thumb, he said, should lie along the shaft slightly to the right of center. Armour advocated a right-hand grip with the club held essentially in the fingers (as all top players have and do) and the V of the thumb and forefinger pointing to the right shoulder.

Armour used and prescribed a stance with both feet turned outward. For the drive, he favored a closed stance (the right foot withdrawn 3 or 4 inches behind the left); for the long irons a square stance (both feet even with a line parallel to the intended line of flight); and for the short irons an open stance (right foot advanced 3 to 4 inches ahead of the left). Here again he went along with the general thinking of his time.

In some important areas of the golf swing, Armour placed himself in opposition to certain later theorists, and Hogan in particular.

You must have the hips in position to turn easily. Tension is set up when the hips are locked. That's what accounts for the majority of bad shots under tournament pressure. . . . A great many players turn their shoulders and think that their hip action is correct. What they don't realize is that you can turn the shoulders while keeping the hips fixed, but when you turn the hips the shoulders go along.

(Hogan, of course, said that retarding the turn of the hips was a must, and added in this connection: "Let the shoulders turn the hips.") "The cardinal principle of all golf shot-making is that if you move your head, you ruin the body action," said Armour. Hogan said that moving the head was the result, not the cause, of faulty body action.

Armour perhaps comes closest to being a radical golf theorist in his conception of the conscious role that the hands play in the golf swing. Basically it is that the left hand merely controls and positions the clubhead on the downswing and that the hit is a "lashing action" with the right hand. "On your long shots," he said, "hit the ball with the right hand just as hard as you can while keeping the body steady. . . ." The idea of the steady body seems to be Armour's alone—unique with him, or very nearly so. The reader might wonder, in the light of statements by so many other experts that the lower body at impact should be moving swiftly forward and turning, whether Armour really meant that the body should be held "steady" in the hitting segment of the swing. He clearly did, as evidenced by his explanation that follows:

The reason for keeping the body steady is plain, if you'll stop and think. You can reason it out in the following logical steps:

You know you must have clubhead speed to make the ball move far.

Your hands are holding the club; therefore, your hands are the main elements in making the clubhead move. Your body and arms could remain in fixed positions, yet your hands alone could hit the ball a crisp blow.

The faster your hands move, the faster the clubhead is going to move.

But if your body is moving ahead, too, the relative speed of your hands will be diminished.

Therefore, to get the greatest speed of the clubhead, you must get the greatest speed of your hands, and that can't be secured unless your body is on a steadily fixed, upright axis.

This line of reasoning recalls Vardon and his advocacy of having the left leg "stiffen to the point of rigidity" as the ball is hit. Armour gives no such advice with regard to the action of the left leg, but a rigid left leg would produce the effect that Armour called for.

Armour concluded his dissertation on the full swing with the advice that there should be a definite pause at the top of the backswing. A pause before starting the downswing, he said, would infinitely improve the timing of most golfers.

Theorists at Odds

There have been many well-regarded teachers of golf who were not outstanding players but who, through either superior logic or plausibility, or both, established themselves as highly regarded theorists. Other things being equal, the golf buff prefers to learn from a man like Tommy Armour, whose tournament exploits were more than sufficiently lustrous to stamp him as a person who should have known what he was talking about. But if any teacher is positive enough and highly articulate, he well may command equal attention with the name player. All golfers, not excepting the very best, tend to believe that somewhere, somehow there is a simple formula for hitting a golf ball straight, long, and accurately. One who said that he had such a formula, and said it with such conviction that he could claim to be the most famous teacher in golf, was Ernest Jones.

Jones's playing history is that he was something of a prodigy in England during the years just before World War I. He lost the lower part of his right leg due to wounds suffered in that war, which necessarily limited his career as a player—although he reputedly played remarkably well considering his handicap. He came to the United States in the 1920s and for many years taught in a golf studio at Fifth Avenue and Forty-third Street in New York City. Jones expressed the core of his theory in the simple phrase "swing the clubhead." To illustrate his point, Jones used a device, or gimmick—a pocketknife tied to a string or to one corner of a handkerchief. "I swing the knife and the string is taut because a swinging action always is an expanding action with the weight exerting an outward pull." To further illustrate, he would swing the device along with a golf club, noting that as long as the two stayed together the swing was correct.

Jones was among those earlier theorists who held that the golf swing should form a segment of a circle, with the club retracing the same circular path coming down as going back. He also likened the correct golf swing to the movement of a pendulum.

> *Like a pendulum, it takes the same measure of time to swing (a golf club) irrespective of the length of the swing. Thus, a short putt takes the same measure of time to complete as a full drive, if the same club is used and held in the same place. The idea of swinging fast or slow is not possible in the same length of swing. Therefore, since a true swing takes the same measure of time, the longer the swing the greater the force, or speed.*

In his most popular book, *Swing the Clubhead* (which is the source of the quoted matter above), Jones uses sequence photographs of a five-year-old girl swinging a golf club "perfectly." The child "can swing so beautifully," he says, "because she does not let her imagination interfere with the feel of the clubhead." He was emphasizing his contention that swinging a golf club correctly is an abysmally simple thing, provided the player does not complicate the operation by thinking of extraneous matters like keeping the head still, keeping the left arm fully extended, or moving this or that part of the body. It is hard to reconcile this theory with the experience of, say, Ben Hogan, who said that he first comprehended one important principle of the swing in 1932, another in 1938, and began to think he really understood the swing about 1946, at which time he was thirty-four years old and had been working at mastering the swing for some twenty-two years.

In all golf instruction, oral or written, we find recurring differences of opnion among the authorities as to what is cause and what is effect. A vast majority of experts hold, for instance, that good balance, as provided by a correct stance and proper footwork, is a prerequisite of a good swing. Jones held that a good swing would naturally and automatically produce good balance. Most experts likewise said the hands would function correctly if the body movements were correct and in proper sequence. Jones figured it the other way around. "The sensation of what is done with the clubhead is felt in the hands, which are the medium through which all conscious effort should be directed. All other physical actions of the body follow as a responsive movement . . . forget about the other parts of your body."

Jones went into no great detail about the grip and stance, and the statements he made about them can be described as orthodox. Neither did he make an issue of how the downswing should be initiated. He merely prescribed full reliance on manipulating the hands correctly—and "swing the clubhead."

It was in 1920 that Jones first propounded his theories in writing. They probably had their greatest vogue in the decade preceding World War II and for a few years thereafter. During this period a number of teaching professionals avowedly taught the Ernest Jones Method. Many of them used the knife-on-a-string (or handkerchief) device to illustrate and emphasize the swing-the-clubhead concept. In more recent years, his theories have lost much of their popularity, possibly because golfers found the game rather more complicated than he described it. Actually, the Jones concept was not so much refuted as it was ignored.

In 1967 a golf-swing theorist named Ike S. Handy came out with the highly positive assertion that Jones was not only wrong fundamentally but in fact had the thing figured just exactly backward. According to Handy, who was past fifty when he took up golf and eighty-one when he wrote his book, *How to Hit a Golf Ball Straight*, said unequivocally that Jones and his adherents were swinging the wrong end of the club:

> *They have not told you which end of the club to swing—or, if they did, they told you wrong. The basic theory of it has been "swing the clubhead" and that is precisely the way to miss golf shots. . . . Conversely, the way to hit (golf shots) is by swinging the top end of the club, or by swinging the hands.*

A person cannot, of course, reach a reading audience with a golf book without establishing some credentials. Handy, having started golf at so late an age, had to rely on exploits that become remarkable in the light of his advanced years and the infirmities to which his age makes him a natural heir. It is said of him in his home area of Houston, Texas, that he hits golf shots that are almost invariably straight and soundly struck, lacking only in distance. Whatever his limitations, he does not lack for confidence in the soundness of his theories. And neither does his publisher, Cameron and Company (San Francisco), which presents him as the game's oldest golf prodigy.

Handy goes strongly against a number of long-established golf-swing theories. Principal among them is the theory that the wrists should cock on the backswing and uncock on the downswing. Handy said in effect that this was so much poppy-cock.

Golf theorists from time immemorial have sought to capsule the whole theory of the swing in a sentence or two—if you just do this or that single thing, the rest will follow as naturally and inevitably as the night the day. Handy is certainly no exception: "Only one thing is necessary to hit a golf ball straight. The hands must pass the ball ahead of the clubhead . . . swing your hands—swing the top end of the club."

In presenting the scientific basis for his theory, Handy reaches peak form as an iconoclast. As no other known theorist before him did, Handy says it is not the speed of the clubhead at impact that puts power behind the golf shot. He adduces this theory as follows: "From a scientific standpoint the power which drives a golf ball is the oldest form of force known to man—mass times velocity—and in the case of a golf stroke, plus leverage. It does not increase the velocity of the mass to accelerate the speed of the lever." In effect, Handy is saying that there is no point in increasing the speed of the clubhead beyond the speed at which the body is moving—that to do so, in fact, is worse than pointless because making the clubhead move faster than the body causes the clubface to turn, thereby sending the ball off line. The idea, according to Handy, is not to increase the speed of the clubhead but to decrease it—to make the downswing of the club as slow as possible. He adds that a really good player hitting his best shots does not appear to swing the club at all, but merely to hold onto it and swing themselves, which seems to be about as far from the (Ernest) Jones concept as you can get.

Handy said also that his method is shank-proof, because shanks are caused by letting the clubhead get ahead of the hands, and the ball cannot be shanked if the hands move past the ball ahead of the clubhead.

Curiously, both Jones and Handy, poles apart in their theories, seem to have the same favorite golf author—Sir

Walter Simpson, whose book on the subject appeared in 1887. This is Jones's favorite quotation from it: "There is but one categorical imperative in golf, and that is hit the ball; there are no minor absolutes." And Handy's choice: "Next to the idiotic, the dull, unimaginative mind is best for golf."

Some Early Conclusions and Reflections

It is clear that in beginning our study of the golf swing with Harry Vardon we left out some good players and theorists who preceded him. He must have learned the game from somebody, and he recalled in one of his books that his basic model was sort of a composite of "three or four good amateur players" whose styles he studied and who doubtless also had good models. It may seem arbitrary to leave out virtually altogether such of Vardon's almost equally successful contemporaries as J. H. Taylor, James Braid, and Ted Ray, all of whom unquestionably expressed some thoughts about the golf swing that were both sound and different from Vardon's. I may be guilty of regrettable omissions, but choosing a starting point is necessarily arbitrary. And while I may have left out (or virtually so) some justly famous figures in the Vardon era, I feel that Vardon was justifiably chosen as the spokesman for his time.

Of the contributions that Vardon made to the modern theory of the golf swing, the most far-reaching is that he popularized a grip in which the hands could be made to act as a unit and the fingers of the right hand (in particular) would be on the club. As most knowledgeable golfers know, it is mainly the fingers of the right hand that give the player his sense of touch—in the golfing sense of those terms.

As Tommy Armour and others have pointed out, the clubhead travels some 22 to 26 feet in a full swing, during all but the first foot or so of the backswing the clubhead either is out of the player's line of vision or traveling too fast to be seen with any degree of clarity. The eyes, then, can do nothing to signal the brain that something has gone wrong and needs correction during that critical stage of the swing extending from the backswing takeaway to the start of the downswing. The fingers can and do.

Here I might cite what I always felt was an advantage in stopping the club at the top of the backswing—as I did so pronouncedly in my best years, but hardly do at all now. I think the pause gave me appreciably more time to alter an incipiently wrong swing—either to correct it or improve it—than the nonpause golfer got. I should explain that I did not eliminate the pause deliberately; it just gradually went away, probably because I lost some of the muscular coordination needed to pause at this critical point and still time the swing correctly. I never urged the adoption of the pause on other players, but I think it helped me (as outlined above) .

Getting back to Vardon, I think his overall contribution to golf theory was enormous. If he was wrong—or partially wrong—on some points, he was certainly right on some other and highly important ones. There also exists the possibility that where he appeared to be wrong he was actually misunderstood. Many golf terms are at best open to different interpretations, even among contemporaries, and the generally accepted meaning of a golf term or phrase can vary widely over a span of fifty or sixty years or so.

Incidentally, Vardon may have been more right than most golfers would think in his statement that the weight should be evenly or equally distributed on both feet as the clubhead meets the ball. Some tests were conducted in California a few years ago to determine as nearly as possible the relative distribution of the golfer's weight at impact, and certain very long hitters—notably George Bayer—were shown to have about as much weight on the right foot as on the left as the clubhead came through the hitting area. Most leading players, however, make a point of saying that the bulk of the weight should be shifted to the left side in the early stages of the downswing.

It might be interesting and instructive to imagine an adjustment of time that would permit a threesome comprising the Vardon of 1900, the Bobby Jones of 1930, and the Ben Hogan of 1960 to play 18 holes together and follow the round with a convivial drink or so and a discussion of the theoretical aspects of the golf swing. Would Vardon or Jones see in Hogan new possibilities for bettering their swings and change them accordingly? Would Hogan see something in their swings that he had overlooked? And so on. Whatever the answers to these questions, I would sure like to make it a foursome. And I would more than gladly buy the drinks as long as any of them wanted to stay around and talk golf.

I have pointed out some seeming contradictions between Jones and Hogan. The paradox that may strike the readers as most nearly irreconcilable has Jones saying that the ball is not and should not be hit from the inside out and Hogan saying it must be. Actually, I would say that the two men were far closer than their statements make them appear to be—at least to the extent that both probably would agree that the ideal path of the clubhead on the downswing could be fairly accurately described as "from slightly inside the line straight through the ball." At any rate, I'm sure that at least part of it gets back to semantics, the ever-present bugaboo of golf instructional writing.

So I must ask the reader to try to be as little confused as possible when he remembers that in their respective primes Jones hit a bit of a hook and Hogan a fade, and that Jones said for the ball to hook it must be hit on the side nearest the player, which implies a clubhead moving into the ball from a point inside the line. Such reasoning can lead only to puzzlement over how Hogan made the ball move from left to right in flight by hitting it from the inside out. But of such is the theory of the golf swing.

According to Hogan's subsequent statements on his hook-proof swing, he hit on the method approximately between the seasons of 1947 and 1948. I recall that it was in 1948 that he told Johnny Revolta that he had finally found a swing that he didn't have to worry about. "I've really got it," he told Revolta. I played with Hogan a great many times that year, and while he won the U.S. Open and several other tournaments, he did not seem to me to be hitting the ball with anything like the authority that characterized his play in later years. He was getting the ball in the hole, as the saying goes, but he was missing a few fairways and having to scramble for pars on some holes, much as the rest of us were doing.

According to my memory, it was in 1950, after the accident, that he began showing us the kind of precision golf that set him apart. I vividly recall his last 36 holes at Merion in the 1950 U.S. Open. I was paired with him that long day, and I kept thinking that he was a far better tee-to-green golfer than I remembered from our many rounds together in 1948. It was in 1950 that he began to take on the miracle-man aura. Small crowds that included a number of his fellow pros would gather around him and try to watch his every move anytime he started hitting out practice balls. Many people had thought that he might never even play golf again, let alone play markedly better than anybody else. Many thought that at least it would take him a while to recapture his old skill, but those of us who knew him well knew that he would not be out there unless he was sufficiently recovered. Right on through 1970, you could be certain that whenever Hogan walked on the first tee at the start of a tournament, he felt himself at least as good a golfer as there was in the field. The same thing will be true if he plays again in competition.

If Hogan was wrong about anything in his theoretical concept of the golf swing, it was in his apparent contention that the muscles around the hips would automatically recoil, or unwind, on the downswing if properly coiled, or wound up, on the backswing. The anatomists say that the muscles do not have the elastic quality that Hogan seemed to attribute to them. The muscles can be stretched, of course, but they stay stretched unless there is positive action taken to make them contract. But you would have to say that if this was an error on Hogan's part, it was a highly technical one.

As to our general theme of each great player's influence on the theory and practice of hitting a golf ball, my guess is that Hogan's will be around for a long time. This guess is based mainly on the fact that he played so superlatively that nobody who ever watched him in his best years can ever forget the experience or forego talking about him whenever golf is the topic of discussion. There is also the fact that what he wrote about the golf swing has been proven to be right in virtually every aspect, even if not always easy to comprehend by the average golfer.

My thought is that Sam Snead was more of a student of the golf swing than his apparent utter naturalness led many to believe. I know from long experience with him that he rarely made the same mechanical mistake twice in any single round. If he hit a bad hook, for instance, he had the trouble diagnosed and the remedy ready by the time he got to the next shot, which bespeaks a considerable knowledge of the workings of the swing. I think it was just that he made the whole thing look so ridiculously easy that the casual observer figured Sam could do it without even thinking about it. As I'm sure Snead would agree, the game isn't quite that easy for anybody.

I have kept a clear mental image of Byron Nelson swinging—an easy thing to do, really, because his swing was both
distinctive and a beautiful thing to watch—but I somehow
thought he gripped the club with his left hand turned more
around to the left and his right hand more on top of the
club—less of a hook grip, so to speak. I guess I thought that
because he normally hit the ball so straight, hooking it only
when that was the most advantageous shot to play.

Upon rereading in 1969 the theories he had expressed in
1946, I had to stop and ponder before realizing that his exceptionally strong sideways thrust of the lower body on the
downswing counteracted any tendency to hook that may have
been inherent in the way he gripped the club.

I noted also that Nelson's peak playing years coincided
with World War II. I had in mind that during those years
he won eleven-straight tournaments and set scoring records
still unsurpassed and unlikely to be. But I'm afraid I left the
impression that Nelson's greatest successes were against
inferior opposition—against fields reduced in overall talent
because many of the best players of the period were not
present. This does not present the true picture. Nelson won
the Masters in 1937, the U.S. Open in 1939, and the P.G.A.
in 1940, during all of which years his opposition was the best
that the world of golf could provide. As noted, he won five
major championships. The other two were the Masters in
1942, in which he beat Ben Hogan in a classic playoff, and the
P.G.A. again in 1945.

There are two possible areas of confusion that I would like
to try to clear up. One statement in particular by Bobby Jones
probably needs some clarification: "The objective of the
player is not to swing the club in a specified manner, nor to
execute a series of complicated movements in a prescribed
sequence, nor to look pretty while doing it, but primarily and
essentially to strike the ball with the head of the club so that
the ball will perform according to his wishes." I refer specif-
ically to the part about executing a series of complicated

movements in a prescribed sequence. I think Jones meant the key word to be "complicated." I'm sure his point was that the swing should be kept as uncomplicated as possible, and not that the sequence of movements, particularly in the down-swing, was unimportant. Jones himself certainly moved the power-generating elements in the prescribed sequence—hips, shoulders, arms, hands—and advocated that other golfers should do likewise. In fact, he looked pretty doing it, but, as he said, that is not important.

It is possible, even likely, that the reader will be confused by Hogan's statements that in his hook-proof swing he opened the clubface to "the widest practical extreme" on the back-swing and that the clubface remained square to the ball (and the intended line of flight) at all times. You have to under-stand that in reference to the backswing the terms "open" and "square" are relative. The same is true of the "shut position" at the top of the backswing.

"Square" means that throughout the backswing the club-face is rotated some 90 degrees but remains square in relation to its beginning position of being aligned squarely with the intended flight of the ball. If you say that the clubface is open at the top of the backswing, you mean that it has been rotated more than 90 degrees within the plane. Any backswing rotation of less than 90 degrees within the plane means that the player who exhibits this technique is a "shut-face" player.

There is always a roll of the clubhead. It is practically a physical impossibility to reach the top of the backswing for a full shot without allowing the left forearm to turn, which means that the clubface turns as an inevitable consequence. The so-called shut-face player simply opens the clubface to a lesser degree than those who keep the clubface square (within the plane) and those who allow the clubface to open (roll) more than 90 degrees within the plane.

The top of a square backswing is characterized by the left wrist's being a straight extension of the left arm and the club's toe pointing some 30 degrees to the left of the target. In the open position, the toe of the club will point to the ground and the left wrist will be cupped in the manner described in the section on Hogan's hook-proof swing—cupped back in the direction of the ball, to put it another way. The shut-face position at the top of the backswing finds the face of the club pointed upward and the left wrist bent in the direction opposite the ball—convex as opposed to the concave position of the left wrist in the open-face method.

The square method is the natural and recommended one. If the player adheres to the fundamentals of a correct swing he will keep the clubface square without giving much conscious thought to the matter. It requires a conscious effort to reach the open position, which, while permitting perhaps freer action of the hands as the clubhead moves through the ball, also requires a better-than-average sense of timing consistently to bring the clubface square to the ball at impact. The inherent difficulty in the shut-face method is that it demands a very big shoulder turn, a bigger turn than is within the physical capabilities of many players. Its advantage, of course, is that it demands less adjustment (or readjustment) to bring the clubface into the ball square with the intended line of flight—less rotation of the clubhead going back and hence less coming down. The shut-face method comes nearest to the mechanical ideal of keeping the clubface aligned with the intended line of flight at all times, which is beyond the physical limitations of the human body. If you think of a simple driving machine, and then of a golfer trying to produce his most powerful blow, you will see the point.

It will almost certainly serve most golfers best to think of starting the clubhead back from the ball square with a straight line to the target and bringing it back down into the ball in the same alignment. Never mind how the clubface may be aligned while it is outside your line of vision. Think instead of where it is (its position) during the various stages of the backswing.

The foregoing is in line with Snead's emphasis on keeping

the golf swing as simple as possible. It also relates positively to Hogan's statement that the player becomes the captive of his own swing once the downswing is launched—that is to say, there is no point in considering how the clubface may be aligned during any stage of the downswing, since no conscious correction is possible.

If you subscribe to Hogan's theories, which would seem to be the most logical thing to do (at least until something new is added to the body of knowledge surrounding the golf swing), you should concentrate principally on those phases of the stroke up to and including the initiation of the downswing by turning the left hip back around to the left. As to the rest of it, you should understand that the clubhead is sort of on its own in the critical stages. Such a thinking process may well help you to swing more freely and naturally—the point being that trying to give thought to something you can't do anything about can only add needless complications to a process best kept simple.

In the above connection, Hogan was recently asked what specific thought went through his mind just before he started his swing. "All I think about is trying to knock the damn ball in the hole," said Hogan.

"Oh," said his questioner. "I thought maybe you used some sort of mental gimmick like starting the club back with your hands, or staying in the backswing plane, or something like that."

"No," said Hogan. "You have to work all that stuff out on the practice tee."

I think this is an indication of just how thoroughly Hogan had worked out the details of his swing and committed them to what he called "muscle memory." I believe, however, that it will help most golfers to have one key thought on which to concentrate at the start of the swing. Thinking of making the takeaway slow and smooth, for instance, can help the player make a better overall swing. The point is to have one positive thought, which, even if it does nothing constructive, may keep negative thoughts from intruding. I think the golfer is getting himself into trouble if he tries to think of more than one phase of the swing while in the process of making it. The ideal is to make the swing completely automatic as far as the various separate movements are concerned, but to do so requires more practice and thought than the average player is able or willing to put in. The swing should be thought out in its entirety before taking the stance, or at least before starting the backswing, but afterward it is best to have no more than a single key thought.

Of Tommy Armour's theories as expressed in his writing, there is one in particular that I just plain do not understand. It is in connection with his statement that the body should be "held steady" in the hitting segment of the swing. "The faster the hands move, the faster the clubhead is going to move," said Armour. "But if your body is moving ahead, too, the relative speed of the hands will be diminished." If I interpret this correctly, by logical extension of the theory it would increase the "relative speed" of the hands if the body were moving backward in the opposite direction from the target in the hitting segment of the swing. Anyway, his logic is bafflling to me, and I can only conclude that maybe he didn't mean it the way it was written.

Neither do I follow the logic of Ernest Jones and his knife-on-a-string business. And between him and Ike S. Handy, I think Handy comes much closer to the mark. In fact, I would say that Handy is right as to the sources of power he advocates using, which can be said to constitute maybe three-fourths of the total power the golfer is capable of producing. But he leaves out an important source of power in theorizing that the wrists should not cock and uncock. And I'm sure that if he can hit the ball as well as he apparently can with his method, he can hit it about a fourth again as powerfully if he adds the cocking and uncocking of the wrists to his swing.

Nicklaus, Player, Palmer

The three golf swings likely to be most widely emulated for the next generation or so belong to Arnold Palmer, Jack Nicklaus, and Gary Player. They are the three players whose accomplishments, styles, and personalities have appealed most to the golfing public since the era of Hogan, Snead, and Nelson.

As the saying goes, such popularity must be deserved, and in this case it surely is. As of this writing, they total twenty-eight major championships and have made enough money to inspire millions of youngsters to look to professional golf as a possible source of great wealth and public adulation. Their major championships include four Masters, two British Opens, one U.S. Open and U.S. Amateur for Palmer; two British Opens, two P.G.A. titles and one each U.S. Open and Masters, for Player; four Masters, three U.S. Opens, two British Opens, three P.G.A. titles and two U.S. Amateurs for Nicklaus.

Of the three, Palmer has been the most wildly and widely admired by the public—an obvious statement in light of the fact that he has indeed been the most idolized golfer of all time. Nicklaus, who is ten years younger, may now be eclipsing Palmer in popularity. But, both have had and will continue to have a profound effect on the way golf is played. This being the case, the trend of the future is apt to be in the direction of really slugging the ball for absolute maximum distance and away from the smooth-flowing, stylish-looking swing epitomized by Bobby Jones, Sam Snead, and Ben Hogan. These three greats of another era seemed always to have had some power in reserve. Action pictures of them, as well as posed pictures, show them in the classic finish—on balance, hands high, right leg collapsing and bent inward, and so on. Palmer and Player, especially, present quite a different picture at the finish of a shot where maximum distance is the objective. They obviously put every possible ounce of strength and energy into a full shot, and an action picture taken of them at the finish of a swing might show them in any of a number of different positions. Nicklaus finishes on balance with considerably more frequency than either of the other two, but in hitting a full shot he leaves no doubt that he is giving it just about everything he has. If you divided golfers into swingers and hitters, these three would figure to head your list of hitters.

(The omission of Billy Casper or Lee Trevino from this grouping certainly is not meant to imply that they do not rank with these three as players. Billy Casper may in fact be, as some connoisseurs of the game have said, better than any of them, particularly as regards finesse and the ability to adapt his game to any sort of course or weather conditions. At any rate, Casper's techniques will be discussed further on.) Lee Trevino's position in the development at the golf swing is difficult to assess at this time.

A point in common with Palmer and Nicklaus is that both were advised by their first golf teachers to give power priority over accuracy in the beginning stages of learning golf. Both obviously took this advice to heart, and both strongly urge other beginning players to follow the same principle. As is well-known, Palmer's first teacher was his father, Deac Palmer, and Nicklaus's was Jack Grout, then the professional at the Scioto Country Club in Columbus, Ohio. "Hit it hard," both boys were told, and hit it hard they always have. Power hitting came quickly and naturally to Palmer and Nicklaus, both of whom were exceptionally strong as boys. Player, much smaller than the other two, had to work harder for the power he needed to become a champion. He never became as long a hitter as his two arch-rivals, but he eventually learned to hit it out there with all but the very longest hitters.

Naturally enough, the golf-swing theories espoused by these three coincide to a considerable degree. It would, however, be unwieldy to present separately their points in common and their differences, so we will instead present separately the basic theories of each, avoiding repetition as best we can.

Nicklaus

Jack Nicklaus is an individualist and very much his own man in the matter of golf theory as in everything else. He is fully aware, for instance, that his swing is characterized by what is known as a flying right elbow—something that golf teachers tell their pupils to avoid. Characteristically, he freely admits it and stoutly defends it. He explains it as part of the modern theory of golf.

> *Golf is different today. This is the era of the power golfer. You see more and more of the young players employing the modern power swing. The arc is very wide going back. While the right elbow doesn't exactly "fly," it*

*isn't tucked in as tightly as it once was. I probably exagger-
ate the elbow-away-from-the-body move more than any
other player, but the difference is only a matter of degree.
All the young power players have the elbow out a bit, since
it permits a wider arc, and . . . the increased leverage a
wide arc creates is a much more trustworthy means of gain-
ing clubhead velocity than speeding up your hands, no
matter how strong they are.*

Jack thinks Hogan is in a class by himself but does not
blink at expressing, with positiveness equal to Hogan's, different theories in regard to certain facets of the swing.

*You cannot make a full shoulder-turn (on
the backswing) unless you make a full hip-turn. If you
inhibit your hips from turning, you'll inhibit your shoulders
from turning. The amount of hip-turn in a golfer's swing
is governed by three things: the length of the club, the
width of the stance, the position of the feet and legs. The
second, the width of the stance, is quite simple. If a golfer
widens his stance, it restricts his hip-turn. Bob Jones, to
cite one example, used a very narrow stance to facilitate the
freest hip-turn of any golfer of the 1920s. This set up his
full, rhythmic swing and was the source of the power that
made Jones, when he wanted distance, one of the longest
wooden-club players of his time.*

Hogan, of course, said it was vital to inhibit the hip turn,
although he used the term "retard" instead of "inhibit."
Hogan said also that the turning of the shoulders both produced and regulated the turning of the hips. Nicklaus put it
just the other way around.

We likewise find Nicklaus and Hogan theoretically apart
in the matter of the position of the hands at the top of the
backswing. Nicklaus says get them "as high as you can," while
Hogan emphasized that between getting the hands above or
below the backswing plane established at address, it is better
to have them below this plane.

Like all top-rung golfers, Nicklaus places great stress on

maintaining good swing tempo. His way of doing this, and which he recommends for others, is to make the start of the backswing literally as slow as possible. It is his theory that the golfer's natural tendency is to increase the tempo of the swing as it progresses and that a "ridiculously slow" start will avert the danger of making the swing hectic and jerky later on.

Since Nicklaus's swing produces such exceptional power, golfers study it with a view to discovering the sources of that power. He says that the first consideration is to have a club of the proper weight and balance. This is, of course, an individual matter, but Jack's experience indicates that a considerable number of golfers might be trying to swing a driver that is too heavy for them. After considerable experimentation, Jack settled on a driver that has an overall weight of 14 ounces, an S (for stiff) shaft, and a swing-weight of D–1.

Pictured here, and on the following four pages, Jack Nicklaus as he appeared early in his career. He has slimmed down considerably but maintained his powerful swing.

Just as a matter of personal preference, he had three very slight alterations from standard specifications built into his driver. It is a fourth of an inch shorter than the standard 43 inches, has a 9-degree face-loft instead of the usual 10 or 11 degrees, and grip-size (circumference) just a fraction larger than standard. These three deviations are noted as a matter of interest and would be of little or no importance to another golfer trying to choose a driver of the proper weight and balance for himself.

The basic specifications of Nicklaus's driver probably should, however, be worth consideration by other golfers, as would his reasons for settling on them. In his amateur days, he used a driver with a considerably heavier swing-weight—D–5 or D–6. He also experimented with an X (for extra-stiff) shaft. And for a time he tried a driver weighing 13 ounces overall. He came down to the lesser swing-weight after noting that swinging so heavy a clubhead tended to tire him and change his swing tempo, particularly on a day when he had to play 36 holes. He went back to the S shaft from the X shaft simply because he found the X was not right for him. With the 13-ounce club, he tended to swing too fast, especially in the early stages of the round. So his eventual selection was largely a matter of trial and error. It would seem that the average golfer should choose a driver with a lesser swing-weight, a more flexible (whippier) shaft, and a lighter overall weight. And also in a general way, this is true. But actually, personal preference, or individual suitability, enters the choice. A club that does not feel good in the player's hands is not the one for him, no matter how scientifically chosen. The main point is that having a driver that is "right" for you is highly important, as evidenced by Jack's putting it first on the list of the "four sources of power."

No doubt the best, and certainly the simplest, way to choose your driver (and your other clubs as well, of course) is through consultation with a competent professional who knows your swing. Nevertheless, it will be helpful to both you and your professional if you know something of the factors involved. For one thing, you will be happier to accept his advice if you understand the basis of it. And since Nicklaus stressed the importance of the subject, I will include some of the basic facts about it here.

Professionals and amateurs alike mostly go by swing-weight in judging the suitability of a club for a given player. There is logic in this, but it can also be tricky. The factors in swing-weight are the overall weight of the club and the location of the club's balance point (center of gravity) —meaning the point on the shaft of the club from which the weight above and below are equal. The nearer the clubhead this balance point is located relative to the overall length, the greater the swing-weight. For instance, if you wanted to increase the swing-weight without increasing the overall weight, you would have to add weight to the part below the balance point and subtract weight from the part above it. In so doing, you would, of course, slightly increase the flexing characteristics of the shaft. (Nicklaus, for example, got a slight relative stiffening of his driver shaft and lowered the swing weight by approximately a point (D-2 to D-1) by shortening the club by a quarter of an inch. The change in the swinging characteristics of the club was small indeed, but for Nicklaus it changed the feel of the club.)

Men's clubs normally range in overall weight from 12½ to 14½ ounces. Shafts normally are marked for flex to denote regular, stiff, or extra-stiff. The normal swing weight is from D-0 to D-8. Some combination within these ranges will suit virtually all players. You are advised herewith to go more by "feel," supplemented by some testing, in choosing a club of the proper weight and balance for you. (Women and junior players will want somewhat lighter clubs with slightly more flex in the shafts.)

To get on with Nicklaus's three other basic sources of power, he lists second a wide backswing arc. As noted earlier, he theorizes that the width of the arc can be increased—or a maximum arc facilitated—by letting the right elbow move out from the body on the backswing. In assessing this theory, the aspiring power hitter should understand that a wide back-swing arc is in itself completely without merit or effect, except insofar as it helps to ensure that the club swung to the top of the backswing with a full turn of the shoulders and not by just pulling the left arm across the chest. What is wanted, is a full extension of the left arm throughout the backswing, plus a full turn of the shoulders, and the golfer whose objective is maximum power should accomplish these ends by the most practicable means.

Going on to Nicklaus's point No. 3, he emphasizes that at the top of the backswing the player should have a feeling of stored-up tension—of the body being wound up, coiled, ready and eager to spring into the downswing. In his particular case, he feels this tension on the inside of his right foot, the inside of the flexed right knee, and inside his right thigh. "I begin my downswing," he says, "by pushing off the right foot with the right knee, and my right thigh drives me forward." Sequence pictures of him show that in the process of starting the downswing he brings his right elbow back in close to the body so that it is pointing to the ground.

In Jack's description of point No. 4—the actual act of hitting the ball—the discerning reader will see touches reminiscent of Harry Vardon and Bobby Jones (the firming of the left side), and of Ben Hogan (the left hip rotating swiftly back around). But the mixture of these elements is according to Jack's own prescription, and I will set it down as described by him in his most recent book, *The Greatest Game of All*, in which his collaborator was Herbert Warren Wind, who also was Hogan's collaborator in the latter's *Modern Fundamentals of Golf*.

> *The first push forward on the downswing is succeeded by a whiplash motion that results when your left leg firms up and your left hip moves out of the way as you enter the hitting zone. Let me describe this slowly. On that*

first push forward, your hips move forward—laterally. Your shoulders have begun to move, coordinated with the hips. At this point in the swing, your arms are just beginning to start down from the top—they haven't moved much at all compared with your hips and shoulders. You're moving the upper part of your body—the hips and shoulders—faster than the arms can move. Accordingly, at this stage of the downswing your arms need an added acceleration, "more throttle," in order to catch up. What happens is this. As your hands are about to enter the hitting zone, your hips stop moving forward and start to turn, to spin, to the rear. The speed of your body is slowed down by the turning of the hips, and this produces a slinging action in which your arms, your hands, and the clubhead are released with such speed that they do catch up with your body as you hit through the ball. The faster you can move your hips forward and then whip them out of the way, the faster will be your slinging action—an action that continues well past impact, with the arms reaching full extension only after the ball has been struck.

The controlling factor for me on this vital phase of the downswing is my left side. Let me be more specific. After I have made the initial push forward off my right foot, right knee, and right thigh, my hips move laterally and my weight shifts to my left side. When I feel that the bulk of my weight has been transferred to my left side—actually it hasn't been, but it feels that way for every golfer—then I want my left hip to brake its forward motion. I do this by firming my left leg with a conscious movement—firming the left knee. The left leg becomes almost straight but it retains its flexibility. This act of firming the left leg forces the left hip to rotate to the rear—what is commonly called "clearing the left side." I have very strong legs and thighs, and so I am able to turn the left hip out of the way very, very fast. This is the principal reason, I think, why I am able to generate a great deal of clubhead speed and to hit the ball longer than most golfers.

When Jacks says that very late in the downswing he brakes the forward motion of his left hip by a firming of the left leg with a "conscious movement—firming the left knee," I'm sure he means that he consciously programs this movement into his swing before he starts. He can hardly mean that at this critical stage of the swing he has a separate conscious thought and acts on it. The action at that point—Jack's action in particular—is taking place far too swiftly for such a thought-act process to be carried out. I make this point to keep the reader from drawing a wrong conclusion as to how the "conscious movement" takes place.

The point on which I most thoroughly agree with Jack is that he is indeed very strong in the legs and thighs, that he is able to turn the left hip out of the way very, very fast, and that this is the principal reason why he can generate the clubhead speed that makes him such a long hitter.

On the "don't" aspects of the swing, Jack also lists four main points, or principal errors that wreck a swing. They are a bad grip, bad alignment, a bad head position during the swing, and a bad, jumpy rhythm leading to bad timing.

In Nicklaus's view, the hardest full shot in golf, and one that rarely, if ever, is even attempted, is one in which the player aims straight at the target and tries to keep the ball from moving either left or right—in short, the straight shot. Jack himself is essentially a fader, a left-to-right player, except, of course, when the special conditions of a shot demand a hook or draw. Thus he obviously considers the left-to-right technique superior to the right-to-left technique, but ranks the latter method ahead of the straight-at-the-target technique.

He figures, as do many other players (but by no means all), that the player gives himself a greater margin for error if he starts with the thought that he is going to make the ball move left to right—hopefully by just the amount calculated but to some degree, in any event. Here is his explanation of the theory:

> Say I'm playing a 5-iron shot to a green 80 feet wide, with the pin positioned in the center of the green. If I aim at the pin, that leaves me only 40 feet on either side if I hook or slice the shot. As a left-to-right

player, I give myself a much greater margin for error if I aim 20 feet to the left of the pin and try to work the ball in. I can make a 40-foot error and still keep the ball within 20 feet of the hole. The same in reverse would apply for the right-to-left player, of course.

Assuming that a golfer has learned how to fade or draw the ball—whichever is the most dependable method for him—10 percent of the time he will make a mistake and his fade or draw won't come off, but the percentages are with him. Furthermore, golfers make much freer and better swings when they're playing for an area; they know they have ample margin for error and they go about their shots in a relaxed manner. It is significant, I think, that the two most consistently accurate shotmakers the game has known, Harry Vardon and Ben Hogan, didn't try to bisect the fairway or split the pin, but being left-to-right players, they aimed to the left of their target and let the ball fall in.

Speaking for myself, when I'm playing left-to-right really well, off the tee I allow for the ball to swing half the width of the fairway. I aim for the left edge of the fairway, so that if my fade doesn't come off, I'll still be in the fairway and not in the rough. With a 3-iron, I'll aim about 20 to 30 feet to the left of the flag; with a 5-iron, 15 or 20 feet to the left; with an 8-iron, about 10 feet; with a wedge, just a shade to the left. It's harder, of course, to fade or draw a short iron, intentionally or unintentionally, than a long iron or a wood.

Nicklaus's strong advocacy of the fade naturally raises the question of how he brings it off. To put it simply, he says he just opens the clubface a bit at address and swings as for a straight ball. Generally speaking, he opens the clubface at approximately the same angle on all full shots, seeking about the same degree of spin each time. The longer the shot, of course, the more the ball will move left-to-right, his fade being gradual over the entire flight of the ball.

He considers this method simpler, more reliable, and therefore better than such fade-inducing adjustments as gripping with the left hand turned more around to the left and the right hand more on top of the club (the weak grip) ; and in particular, better than deliberately bringing the clubhead into the ball from outside the line to inside the line.

Nicklaus recognizes that a golfer who has accustomed himself to the draw-hook right-to-lcft stylc of play would find it hard to revamp his swing and become a fader, and he does not advise that such a change be attempted. He does, however, advise beginners, young ones especially, to work toward being left-to-right players as soon as they achieve some mastery of the fundamentals.

Notes and Comments on Nicklaus

Jack Nicklaus and I are next-door neighbors in Lost Tree Village, Florida. Our homes there are hard by the first fairway of the Lost Tree Country Club golf course. We visit back and forth, and our conversations often touch on both the theoretical and reminiscent aspects of golf. We sometimes play Lost Tree together, but not as much as might be supposed, because Jack is more tennis player, fisherman and family man than golfer when he's home. I have played with him in tournaments, in practice rounds before tournaments, and have often watched him in tournaments where he was a contender and I a television commentator. I cite these things not to call attention to my close association with one of the great players in the game's history, but to establish a basis for commenting at some length on his golf game. I have also read much of what he has written about golf.

The mathematically minded reader may question the figures Jack cites in support of his contention that by being a fader he gives himself a greater margin for error than he would otherwise obtain. Take, for instance, his illustration: With a 5-iron he can aim 20 feet to the left of the hole and count on being no more than 20 feet to one side or the other if he makes a 40-foot error. This presupposes the shot will range from straight to fading 40 feet in flight. But the player who aims straight at the pin likewise has the same 40-foot margin for error, assuming that in his effort to hit the ball straight he may err 20 feet to one side or the other—40 feet in all.

There is one other seeming fallacy in Jack's theory. He says, rightly, that by opening the clubface at address the effective loft of the club is increased. Thus, by his own calculations, a 4-iron becomes a 5-iron, and so on, for purposes of choosing a club for a shot of a given distance. But, again by Jack's logical calculations, the ball will go farther on those occasions when the clubhead comes into the ball square to the line toward the selected target and produces a straight shot. And by the same line of reasoning, the 40-foot (maximum) fade will cut down on the straight-line distance the ball will cover. So the fader in effect adds to the problem of making his overall distance come out right.

In the 1969 Masters, Jack put an uncommon number of iron shots over the left side of the green. His swing during that period was off just enough so that he was hitting the ball straight instead of getting the controlled fade for which he allowed and on which he depended. All golfers' swings vary from day to day, of course, including Jack's. Both the habitual right-to-left player and the habitual left-to-right player may find himself hitting the ball straight on a given day, despite using what seems to him the same swing as usual. Likewise, either type may find himself drawing or fading the ball more than he usually does without being aware of any marked change in his normal swing. In these not infrequent situations, most golfers will try to adapt early in the round, in recognition of and resignation to the fact that golf is a game of constant correction and minimization of errors. On this point, Jack is more stubborn than most. If he thinks a shot calls for a certain flight pattern of the ball, he tries to make it conform to that pattern. He fights against giving in to what might be called the vagaries of his swing.

Any other golfer's assessment of Jack Nicklaus is bound to be colored by the fact that he has accomplished so much so quickly (all those major championships and the top of the all-time money-winning list before age thirty-five and yet retained such great potential. One tends to envision a combination of Jack's power and natural talent and Ben Hogan's deep knowledge of the game and capacity for hard work. An analogous situation exists in almost any golf club. The short-hitting, cagey player looks at the long-hitting player of roughly equal handicap and thinks, "Boy, if I could hit the ball that far I could beat anybody." But no player has ever combined the power of a Nicklaus with the finesse of, say, a Hogan or a Billy Casper. There are a few tour players—two or three, maybe—who drive the ball farther than Jack does and who hit an 8-iron where Jack would hit a 6 or 7, but none of them has so far been able to integrate power with finesse to the extent that Jack has.

It is a logical supposition that Jack may one day become a better golfer than anyone else ever was. I remember that when Jack played so flawlessly and powerfully in lowering Hogan's record for the Masters by three strokes in 1965, Bobby Jones said, "The kind of game Jack Nicklaus played out there this week is one I am not familiar with," meaning that Jones himself was astounded at such a display of talent. Jack is capable of hitting shots of which all the other players I know are incapable. For instance, on the eighteenth hole at the Westchester Country Club in the New York City area he hit a 3-wood shot that cleared a tall tree in front of him and carried in all some 290 yards to the green. There are a few players on the tour who can hit the ball that far, and quite a large number who can get up high enough that quick with a 3-wood to have cleared the intervening tree, but none, I think, who can do the two things in combination.

It seems unlikely that Jack will subsequently be able to

swing the clubhead faster than he presently does. He may, however, work out a reliable system by which he can hit the ball farther by hitting it straight away or drawing it instead of fading it, while at the same time keeping it under control. There is no reason to suppose that in doing so he would lose the fading technique. It would just be a matter of adding more shots to his repertoire. If so, the advantage he already has in being able to outhit almost everybody else—of being able to reach those crucial par-5 holes in two when others can't, and hit shorter irons into the par-4 and par-3 holes—will be appreciably increased.

I recently wrote a sort of critique of Jack's swing for *Golf Digest* in which I intimated that in certain stages of his swing he got himself in trouble from which he could escape only because of his exceptional strength and far-above-average muscular coordination. These are qualities he is apt to retain for some years to come, and if he couples them with a more simplified swinging technique and continues to add to his already formidable knowledge of the game, he will doubtless realize the even greater success predicted for him.

It will be noted that the elements Nicklaus thinks of as being used to initiate the downswing are all on the right side —a pushing off the right foot with the right knee and a forward drive provided by the muscles of the right thigh. Others, notably Hogan, said that the downswing should be started by a turning of the left hip back around to the left. This is one of those seeming contradictions that are essentially not contradictory. Being altogether right-handed, Jack tends to think of movements as being initiated from the right side. Hogan, being basically left-handed, figures to have a different sense of how a movement is started. Actually, their overall movement incorporated in the downswing start is quite similar.

Following a similar line of reasoning, Nicklaus and Hogan are not actually far apart in the matter of how much the hips should turn on the backswing. Nicklaus, with his stocky build, probably can turn his hips without straining and still not turn them very far. Other, more supple golfers will find it useful to retard the hip turn by squaring the right foot at address, as Hogan prescribes.

Gary Player

Next to Ben Hogan, Gary Player is probably the hardest-working, most dedicated golfer the game has known. He worked long to develop a sound swing, made a thorough study of both the mechanical and mental aspects of the game, and is unceasing in his efforts to stay in the best possible physical condition.

Despite the amazing fact that he parred the first three holes he ever played, Player is not as liberally endowed with natural talent as, for instance, Arnold Palmer or Jack Nicklaus. He lacked their physical attributes, but through daily exercise and strict attention to his diet, he became a very strong young man indeed. Also, Player comes about as close as a man can to thinking golf constantly, except for periods during which he goes back to his home in South Africa to rest.

Typical of him is the procedure he followed during the 1965 United States Open at Bellerieve Country Club in St. Louis, which he won to become the third player in the history of golf to have won all four of the game's major championships. (Gene Sarazen and Ben Hogan preceded him, and Jack Nicklaus later became the fourth member of this ultra-select group.) As soon as he woke up in the morning, Player began to do things at a deliberately slowed-up, unhurried pace—dressing, breakfasting, driving leisurely to the golf course and arranging to arrive there with time to spare, pausing longer than usual between shots while warming up on the practice range, and so on. He was gearing himself to the pace, or tempo, that he wanted to maintain throughout the day's round. As Player well knew, the pressures in any major tournament are enormous, and this one was particularly important to him. Some years before, he had announced that his goal in golf was to win all of the four major championships, and in winning this one he could realize that lifetime ambition. He knew that he would be more than ordinarily subject to pressure and might speed up his swing and become hurried and harried when he needed to be just the opposite. Hence the elaborate preparations to gear his thoughts and acts to an unhurried pace.

Just incidentally, there is quite a good lesson here for all golfers. Your average player, of course, will rarely want to prepare for his round as seriously and elaborately as would a man in Player's position. But a modified version of Player's approach can be most rewarding in terms of lower scores and the naturally consequent greater enjoyment of the game. At least try to avoid rushing around and getting yourself in a dither. Arrive at the course with a few minutes to spare. If you hit some warm-up shots, as you should if at all possible, remember that it is far better to hit twenty balls with a leisurely pause between swings than forty balls hurriedly.

Player turned professional in his eighteenth year. Three years later he had a sufficiently impressive record to be invited to the Masters. In his formative years as a golfer he ran the gamut of grips. At first he had the left hand turned so far over to the right that he could see all four knuckles looking down at the address position, and the right hand well under the shaft—the ultra-strong, ultra-hook grip. With such a grip, he naturally lacked accuracy. Then he observed British professional Dai Rees, who at the time had the very weak, fade-slice grip—no knuckles at all visible on the left hand, and the right hand turned well around to the left and on top of the shaft. Impressed by Rees's accuracy, Player adopted that grip. And with it he gained much in accuracy but lost much in distance.

When Player first competed in the Masters—which is

where I first met him—he was an impressive player but definitely not a long hitter. Being unable to reach the Augusta National's par-5s in two, he was giving away too many strokes to the many players there who could. Realizing that he had overcorrected, he adopted a standard grip—two knuckles of the left hand visible and the V's formed by the thumb and forefinger of both hands pointing about to the right eye. Even before he won the Masters in 1961, he had gained as much as 30 to 40 yards on his drives and was hitting those par-5s in two with a frequency at least comparable to that of the top players. He had a very wide backswing arc, giving him a full shoulder turn, and he was getting a full extension through the ball. In short, he was swinging much as he does today.

As would be expected, the golf idol of Player's youth was his fellow South African Bobby Locke. Locke, a four-time winner of the British Open and a most successful campaigner on the P.G.A. tour in the United States in the late 1940s and early 1950s, was almost certainly the greatest player who ever lived who hooked every shot, from the drive on down through the short irons. He probably is, to some degree, responsible for Player's starting out as a hooker. If Player's early style was modeled on Locke's, he changed it soon after he began competing on an international scale. But at least as late as 1956, Player spoke of Locke in a manner that can only be described as reverent. "The best," Player would say of Locke, "the very best."

In more recent years, Player was critical of Locke's swing—if not of his entitlement to first place in the list of the great golfers of history. "Locke took the club back inside the line too quickly and too much," Player said. "He was a great player, but could have been a greater one if he had developed a better and straighter takeaway."

Above, and on the following three pages, Gary Player demonstrates
the solid swing that made him a constant winner.

Player did not, however, lose sight of certain highly valuable lessons implicit in Locke's style of play. Locke was a master strategist. He never hit a foolish shot and rarely one that could be called unwise. From a scoring standpoint—which is what really matters—he extracted the absolute maximum from the talent he possessed. In the matter of weighing a shot's inherent risks against the probable rewards and acting accordingly, Locke probably stands alone as the greatest (one always tends to note Hogan as a possible exception in any such statement as the foregoing). Also, and perhaps more important, Locke exemplified the vital importance of being able to get down in two from around the green—a pitch or chip and one putt. Watching him—or better still, playing with him—one could see how a good short game worked to the betterment of the long game, giving the player greater confidence and affording him a wider range for strategic decisions: whether to aim for the pin, the middle of the green, or to insure that in the event of missing the green the resulting position would offer a relatively easy chip or pitch. And, of course, Locke was a genius with the putter. He so rarely missed a putt from 6 feet or less that he could play a round looking like he was shooting an 80 and come coasting in with a 69. And on those not infrequent days when he was hitting the ball well and giving himself some reasonable putts for birdies, he kept wasted opportunities to a minimum.

So it is, to a considerable extent, with Player. He hits the ball better than Locke did and is comparable with him as a strategist, par-saver, and capitalizer on available birdie opportunities. Player's concept of the golf swing is basically similar to Hogan's, with a few personal modifications. He stresses a full turn of the shoulders and a stance with the right foot squared and the left foot turned out by some 20 degrees. His method of triggering the downswing is an immediate shifting of the weight back to the left side. This, he says, is the key point on which he concentrates. "The weight shift to the left side adds distance because it helps delay the uncocking of the wrists on the downswing. This 'delayed hit' uncocks the wrists just before impact so that the speed of the clubhead really accelerates as it meets the ball."

Unlike his good friend and rival Jack Nicklaus, Player is stoutly against letting the right elbow get out and away from the body on the backswing. "I like to imagine my right elbow is against my side at address," he says, "although physically it isn't. I want this elbow tucked into my side as soon as possible on the downswing, so that what I'm doing at address is what I hope to duplicate at impact.

Some of the things Player does and advocates for maintaining top physical condition for golf are hardly within the capabilities of most golfers. He does some 75 fingertip push-ups daily, for example, and at least 60 deep knee-bends standing on one leg—30 on each leg. And he stands on his head a minimum of two minutes each day, which he says makes him more alert.

When he was developing his bunker-shot technique, Player would practice sand shots until he holed out at least five times, never leaving the bunker until that fifth one went in. For many of us, I fear, duplicating this feat would frequently necessitate staying in a bunker overnight.

Player obviously has a sound golf swing, as proven by his record, and one whose basic features can be copied with profit. But perhaps more important—for young golfers in particular—he serves as a classic example of what can be accomplished by hard work, clean living, fierce determination, attention to detail, and an indomitable competitive spirit.

Arnold Palmer

Beyond a question Arnold D. Palmer has had a greater influence on the game of golf than any other player. At least in part because of his enormous personal popularity, many thousands have taken up golf, leading to the building of new golf courses, increasing sales of clubs, balls, and dozens of other golf-related items, and bringing golf to or near the top of the list of participant sports. Thousands of youngsters have come to look on professional golf as a possible source of their first million. The Palmer influence has been felt not only in America but in every other part of the world where golf is played.

The greatest beneficiaries of what has been called "The Palmer Appeal" are his fellow players on the P.G.A. tour. Total prize money has more than quintupled since he turned professional in 1954—to the extent that it is now possible to win more than $100,00 in prize money in a year without winning a single tournament—in fact Palmer did it in 1970. While Palmer didn't bring all this about by himself, he did more to bring it about than anybody else.

What Palmer's influence has been and will be on the modern golf swing, as distinguished from the game as a whole, is another question. The Palmer legend is built far more on what he has done than on how, from a technical standpoint, he did it. The millions who have trailed Palmer around courses, and the many more millions who have watched him work his miracles on television, have been much more inclined to exclaim, "Man, what a great shot!" rather than "Man, what a fine swing!" To cite the most obvious contrast, Ben Hogan drew big galleries composed, in large part, of people who wanted to observe his machinelike precision and unparalleled technical skills. People flock to Palmer because they can be fairly certain that he will produce at least a few spectacular shots and occasionally, now, hole some long curling putts before the round is over. To put it another way, with Hogan they tended to watch the swing; with Palmer they watch the ball.

None of this is intended to suggest that Palmer does not have a sound golf swing. Such a proposition would be foolish indeed in light of his record—eight major championships, some fifty-six tournament victories by 1973, more than a million dollars in official prize money, and four times winner of the Vardon Trophy for the lowest scoring average of the year. Palmer has a very sound swing. And more significantly he has a fine all-around game. Proof of this is in the fact that he reached the very top of his profession without ever acquiring a reputation of being the best in any single physical phase of the game. That is to say, he was never the tour's longest driver, most accurate driver, best long-iron, medium-iron, or short-iron player, best chipper, best bunker player, or even the best putter. The point is that he was among the best in all these departments, which, added to his outstanding competitive spirit and the often uncanny ability to reach within himself and produce his best golf when it was most direly needed, made him a great champion.

Palmer was scarcely one to revel in long and involved discussions on the theory of the golf swing. Only once, he says, did he ever accept advice about his own swing from any professional except his father. One of his books on golf is entitled simply *Hit the Ball Hard.* In another how-to-play book —*My Game and Yours*—he devotes 51 pages to the mechanics of the swing and the remaining 107 pages to the mental or psychological aspects of the game. In this connection, he likes to quote his father to the effect that "90 percent of golf is played from the shoulders up." Another of his favorite aphorisms, also given him by his father very early in his golfing life, is, "With a good grip, a little ability, and a lot of desire, anybody can become a good golfer."

It may be reasonably assumed from the above that Palmer takes a simplistic approach to golf-swing theory. The two points he stresses, almost to the exclusion of the rest of it, is that the grip must be correct and the head kept still. And since he says, on the basis of purely personal experience, that the grip is so much a part of being able to make millions and become perhaps the most idolized athlete of an era, let's look closely at what he has to say on the subject:

A powerful and effective swing, demonstrated here and on the three pages following, by one of golf's oldest stars, Arnold Palmer.

There is only one right way to grip a golf club. One must keep both hands locked together and working together, holding the club firmly enough to avoid even the slightest turning in the hands while at the same time leaving the muscles sufficiently relaxed for a nice easy swing—and there is only one way to accomplish this double objective. . . .

As far as the left hand is concerned, it's the last three fingers that do the work. They have to hold the shaft tight against the palm—firmly enough so that it can't turn, yet not so tight as to get cramped and stiff. You lay the shaft diagonally across the left palm, from the base of the index finger to the opposite corner, then close the last three fingers snugly. The forefinger and thumb play a secondary role. They help steady your hold on the club and give you the feel of it.

As far as the right hand is concerned, it's the two middle fingers that do the job. Like the last three fingers of the left hand, they apply the pressure—firm enough to keep the club from turning, but not unnaturally tight. The little finger of the right hand overlaps the index finger of the left hand and forms a link between the two, keeping them working together. The thumb and forefinger of the right hand, like the thumb and forefinger of the left hand, help steady your grip and give you the feel of the club. But it's the middle two fingers that do most of the work. . . . I have heavy calluses running almost the entire length of the two middle fingers, and no calluses anywhere else on the hand.

There's one other thing to watch about the right hand. Notice, if you will, that if you start to close the fingers of your hand, as if about to make a fist, a little pocket forms in the palm; it runs from the heel of the hand—the lower left corner as you look at it—diagonally up toward the base of the index finger. This pocket is very important. When you put your right hand on the club, this pocket must fit over your left thumb. Then the part of your right hand lying below the thumb must close firmly, pressing against the left thumb with a good, snug hold.

If you're holding the club with the last three fingers of your left hand and the middle two fingers of your right hand, and if your left thumb is cradled firmly in that little pocket of your right hand, with the part of the right hand below the thumb keeping a steady pressure, then you've got it.

Palmer notes, of course, that the grip he is describing is the overlapping (or Vardon) grip, and that there is nothing intrinsically wrong with the interlocking and ten-finger grips. The slight changes from standard in these two grips he regards as allowable personal modifications. And on the further assumption that most of the rest of the physical formula for super-success lies in keeping the head still, plus anchoring the feet firmly, let's likewise harken to his view on these matters, going into it feet first, so to speak:

About all you really have to worry about is feeling comfortable. You don't want your feet so far apart that they'll keep you from turning your body smoothly. Nor do you want them too close together, for this also would tie up and restrict your swing. If you just sort of stand up to the ball naturally, you'll find that your stance tends to be about as wide as your shoulders when you're using a driver. Then, as you move down to the shorter clubs, your feet tend of their own accord to move closer together, until they're perhaps no more than 6 inches apart when you're choking the pitching wedge for a little 30-yarder.

As far as the angle of your feet is concerned, they'll be all right if you just get set in the position that seems to be the best balanced, the least awkward. Ordinarily, the way most golfers do it, the left foot is at a slight angle, with the toe pointed out. The right foot is either more or less perpendicular to the line of flight or also pointed out a little. It doesn't matter too much, ordinarily, if the feet are pointed a little more or a little less. Unless a pro tells you that for some perverse reason you have a tendency to hold your feet in a position that ties you up, or have somehow fallen into the habit of doing it—or unless you yourself have noticed that you feel terribly uncomfortable over the ball—you can forget it.

Thus Palmer makes it clear that in his view, getting an essentially correct stance is simple, easy, and largely instinctual.

But, he says emphatically, learning to keep the head still takes considerably more doing. He also emphasizes that there is much more involved in keeping the head still than merely keeping the eyes on the ball:

>It isn't enough just to keep your eye on the ball. You must consciously and deliberately force your head to hold still. And it isn't easy at all. It takes prolonged effort and concentration. It is probably the hardest part of golf to learn. . . . Getting comfortable over the ball is part of it: if you've got a nice balance and your feet are good and firm, you have a far better chance to hold steady. Relaxation is part of it: if your body movements flow free and easy, there's no irresistible physical force to pull you off your axis and make you sway. But it's mostly a matter of concentration: you've got to be determined to hold steady. After that it's a matter of practice. . . . I don't think there is any mechanical method or shortcut in the world which will help you keep your head steady.

Palmer says this in support of his contention that certain contrived gimmicks put forth by others on this vital point are no good. He assigns no value, for instance, to practice swinging while looking in a mirror, or to practicing with your back to the sun so that by watching your shadow, you can see if the head moves.

>You've just got to think about it and practice it until it becomes second nature. Or almost second nature. You can never forget the head entirely. If I didn't keep reminding myself to keep my head steady, I'd go right back to moving it. . . . You'll have to work at it. All I can do is wish you good concentration—and good luck. For if you've acquired a sound grip and then can just manage to keep your head steady, the rest of the mechanical side of golf is a breeze.

In getting at the core of Palmer's concept of the golf swing, we again find ourselves up against the troublesome question of what is cause and what is effect. It has been shown that some notable authorities conceive that if the body functions as it should, the head will not move. Palmer sees it the other way around. He labels as unnecessarily complicated and confusing all writing and discussion about the body turn, pivot, weight shift, and the like. "The swing is the easiest part of golf," he says. "Once you've got the right grip —and if you hold your head steady—it is almost physically impossible to swing badly."

Palmer is clearly in his element when he begins discussing the mental aspects of the game—the winning frame of mind, the capacity for being able to reach down within oneself and come up with the extra effort that turns seemingly inevitable defeat into glorious victory, the belief in miracles that makes miracles happen. This sort of thing is the substance of the Palmer legend.

The legend was largely created in the Masters and U.S. Open of 1960, tarnished slightly in the 1961 Masters, and so fully revived and firmly re-established in the 1962 Masters that it could survive an almost incredible collapse in the 1966 U.S. Open. Here is a brief review: In 1960 he won the Masters with spectacular birdies on the last 2 holes and the Open at Cherry Hills in Denver with a closing 65. In the 1962 Masters he birdied 2 of the last 3 holes to get a tie with Dow Finsterwald and Gary Player, whom he beat in the playoff. In the 1961 Masters, needing only a par on the last hole to win, he took a double-bogey to lose by a shot to Player. In the 1966 Open at the Olympic Club in San Francisco, he led his closest pursuer, Billy Casper, by seven strokes with 9 holes to go, all seven of which strokes he lost on that last 9 by shooting 40 to Casper's 33. Casper beat him in the playoff.

The above facts are cited to show that Palmer, while by no means infallible, can rise to great heights by what is apparently pure willpower and effort. Thus his views about the part that the mind plays in the golf swing must have validity. Palmer appears to get himself all charged up emotionally, like a football player ready to go out or die for dear old Rutgers. But he has a different version: "The mental approach that golf requires is a peculiar and complicated mixture of abiding confidence and patient resignation, of intense concentration and total relaxation." One can see in him the "abiding confidence" and the "intense concentration"—these things he exudes—but I question that anyone watching him would suspect the presence of the two ingredients he labels as "patient resignation" and "total relaxation." In fact, far from seeming patiently resigned, he seems absolutely intent on making something spectacular happen in spite of all odds against it. But he says that all four of the ingredients are there, and he should know. And it probably will come as a surprise to most that he also advises the aspiring golfer to stay "serene."

One myth that exists on the fringes of the Palmer legend is that he just sort of coasts along for the first few holes waiting for a dramatic moment to mount a "charge" and reel off a string of birdies that will give him the sort of sensational subpar score that has come to be expected of him. On the contrary, he says, he tries to concentrate especially hard on the first 3 holes or so, knowing that a good start is important not only in itself but also as a builder of a better and more confident attitude to promote lower scoring through the rest of the round. And, as he points out, the reverse of the proposition is also true. The strokes you lose by a lackadaisical start not only count against you then and there but also tend to throw you off your mental balance for the rest of the round. He does admit that he was inclined to loaf a bit in the early stages when he first became a professional but adds that he quickly corrected the error.

     I know that I myself play my best when I start well," he says. "You won't read about it so often in the newspapers, because it's not as dramatic as a come-from-behind finish, but it's true. In the Masters of 1964, for example, I was tied for the lead after the first round and in front all the rest of the way. I always felt in charge. I felt great, there was never any doubt in my mind that I was going to win. Then there was the Phoenix Open of 1962, which I began with birdies on the first 6 holes. I won that tournament by twelve strokes, the biggest margin I've ever had. That's what a good start can do for you!

You have to keep reminding yourself all the time that the first 3 holes count, for it's easy to forget. Even in an 18-hole round, the whole day seems to loom ahead of you. If you lose the first hole, there's always the second. And if you lose the second hole, too, there are still 16 to go. . . . But if you fall into this lackadaisical mental trap, your day can be ruined before you know it. You're hopelessly beaten in your match; you haven't got a chance of breaking 100 or 90 or 75 or whatever was your goal for the day, and the rest of the round is just a chore and a nuisance. Chalk up another golf round spoiled by carelessness in the early stages.

Palmer has a sort of special mental approach to the last 3 holes, and it, too, is at some variance with the legend. It is not (as in the popular conception of him) that he rouses himself to greater heights of emotion to stage a spectacular finish. Rather, he just makes a special effort to resist any tendency to let down mentally as the end nears—to maintain his normal pace and concentration. He notes that when he made that double-bogey that cost him the 1961 Masters, he did succumb to a mental letdown. He hit a long and perfectly positioned drive off the tee on the Augusta National's par-4 eighteenth, leaving him an easy 7-iron to the big green, and sort of assumed that the par he needed to win would come automatically. He broke out in a big smile that tacitly acknowledged the congratulations that turned out to be so very premature. In a way, he fell victim to a belief in his own image as a man who makes birdies to win tournaments, not double-bogeys to lose them. But it taught him a lesson, and he sees in it a lesson for other golfers as well. The lesson—trite but true—is that the game is on until the last putt drops.

If I ever find myself in a similar situation, with a great drive off the final tee and everybody crowding around to congratulate me, you'll never again see me grinning like a fool at the compliments. I'll say, "Well, now, let's just wait a minute here and see what happens. Nobody wins a tournament until the ball is in the hole and the scorecards signed."

The Putting Stroke

If you have been seriously involved in golf for any considerable length of time, you can observe a player as he steps up to the ball for a full shot and takes his stance and a waggle or two and get quite an accurate idea of how well he plays—whether he figures to shoot in the 70s, 80s, 90s, or higher. There are telltale signs in his movements, too subtle to describe in words but clearly present.

The same thing is by no means true as regards putting. It seems as if there are as many different styles of putting as there are players. Even among the best putters, you see wide stances, narrow stances, closed stances, open stances, square stances, weight mostly on the left foot, weight evenly distributed, weight mostly on the right foot, left elbow out, right elbow out, both elbows out, both elbows in, wristy strokes, arm strokes, and so on ad infinitum. To cite the clearest example that comes to mind, there are Lloyd Mangrum and woman professional Ruth Jessen. Mangrum, one of the half-dozen best putters I ever saw, stands with his feet together, touching. Miss Jessen, also a very good putter, stands with her feet about as wide apart as she can get them without doing a split. All of which is to say that there has been no continuing evolution in the putting stroke in the sense that there has been in the full golf swing. There have been certain putting styles more popular than others during given periods. Judging from old photographs, most of the best players stood more or less facing the hole and positioned the ball opposite the right foot. "Young Tom" Morris, the first of the super-golfers (winner of four-consecutive British Opens beginning in 1868), used this style and popularized it to the extent that it was used by most of the best players for half a century or so after his death, which came soon after he won his fourth British Open. This style also was used, in a less exaggerated form, by Walter J. Travis, the first of the great American amateurs. In more recent years, including the present, the generally basic style is to stand facing at right angles to the intended line and with the ball positioned just inside the left foot.

Yet for all the discrepancies that remain, certain principles have been established. The best putters have been found to have a number of things in common, thus creating what amounts to a body of knowledge about the art of putting. The first principle, obviously, is that the face of the club should be square to the intended line when the ball is struck. From this it follows that it will be helpful if the face of the putter is square to the line for a few inches as it comes into the ball and remains square to the line for a few inches afterward. These points mean almost nothing in themselves, since the face of the putter and the ball remain in contact over a space of about a fortieth of an inch, during which the fate of the putt is decided for good or ill. But the extra inches of having the clubface square do provide a normally needed margin for error.

The second basic principle of effective putting is that the ball should be struck solidly with the putter. Normally, this means that the center of the clubface should hit the center of the back of the ball. This, however, presupposes that the center of the clubface also is the center of its gravity. Some putters, and other clubs as well, have their center of gravity elsewhere than in the center of the clubface—a fraction of an inch or so toward the toe or heel. So we should say that the ball should be struck squarely in that part of clubface where the center of gravity lies—the "sweetspot." Actually, the manufacturers should mark that spot for the player to see as he lines up the clubface with the ball. This is entirely within the rules and would be quite helpful. (Some manufacturers do this, but not always with complete accuracy.) The player can, however, make his own test to find this sweetspot and do his own marking.

The reason a solid blow is required, of course, is that it is the only type that can be relied on to consistently produce the power needed for a given amount of distance. If, for instance, you swing the clubhead just hard (fast) enough to propel the ball 20 feet with a solid blow, an off-center blow will leave the ball 2 to 6 feet short of that distance, depending on the degree of error. The solid blow is the basis of "putting touch"—the sense of being able to hit the ball hard enough to reach the hole and either go in or stop not more than a few inches past.

Paul Runyan, one of the greatest putters in the history of the game, used to devote a considerable portion of his putting-practice time concentrating just on the sound produced as the putter contacted the ball. As all golfers know, there is a particular sound that denotes a solid blow, and Runyan's objective was to achieve consistency in producing this particular click (or clunk) that meant he was hitting the ball solidly.

To consistently hit the ball solidly and with the clubface traveling squarely along the intended line requires that the player keep his body steady. Even a slight movement of the body will cause the clubface to become oriented differently with the ball and, accurate putting being the delicate operation that it is, will generally produce a miss.

The normal tendency, particularly on the shorter putts, is to move the body in the direction of the hole as the clubhead is being brought into the ball. If you miss a lot of putts to the right, you can be pretty sure that this type of sway is at the heart of your trouble. Mostly, I think, this forward movement of the body is caused by anxiety, a desire to "help" the ball along its way to the hole. The tendency also may be augmented by the fact that on other shots the middle part of the body does move laterally in the direction of the target and the weight is shifted to the left side.

At any rate, the better golfers are continually trying to build into their putting stroke a method of bracing themselves, so to speak, against movement of the body during the putting stroke. It is always chancy to write that a given player has a certain putting style or uses a certain type of putter, because both these things are subject to change without notice. You can state that this or that player stands with his feet fairly widely spaced and uses a blade-type putter and the next day see him putting with his feet together and using a mallet-head. There are some, however, who stick with the same basic style over the years. Arnold Palmer, for instance, has long been identified with this somewhat contorted stance: both knees turned strongly inward and almost touching and the toes of both feet also turned inward—sort of knock-kneed, pigeon-toed. This is in line with Palmer's overall theory that the head must be kept still at all costs and that the rest will follow. What he is doing is trying to anchor himself over the ball and reduce the chance of head (or body) movement to an absolute minimum.

Quite a number of players take a putting stance with a preponderance of weight on the left side—the theory being that if the weight is mostly on the left foot to begin with, there will be less of a tendency to shift it to that side during the putting stroke. Others simply try to balance the weight equally on both feet and maintain this balance. Jack Nicklaus normally puts a little extra weight on the right side, figuring this to be his own best method of guarding against body movement. Jerry Barber, always ranked high in any list of golf's best putters, perfected a style distinguished by the left arm bent so that the elbow pointed toward the hole—or parallel to the intended line. Jim Ferrier, another great putter, positions his right elbow much as Barber does the left. In both instances the idea is to provide a brace for an almost pure hinged-wrist stroke. The styles of these veteran players naturally call to mind Leo Diegel, a great player of an earlier era, who pointed both elbows outward as a sort of double brace for the same type of hinged-wrist stroke used by Barber and Ferrier. I am told that Diegel was the first of the top-flight players to develop a sort of mechanized putting stroke, as differentiated from the more natural, or touch, method in general use up to and during his time. Diegel was one of the very best shotmakers of his era (he won a number of tournaments in the decade following World War I, including the P.G.A. in 1928 and 1929), but he was a nervous man and inclined to extreme jumpiness on the greens. As so many golfers have, he was looking for a putting stroke that would minimize the effects of jumpy nerves, a condition usually called the "yips."

According to some researchers of golf history—and my own observations as well—the very best putters over the years have been what I would characterize as pattern putters. That is to say, they followed a largely set and timed routine in lining up the putt, approaching the ball, taking the stance, and making the stroke. Thus it is probably more than coincidence that the player who most closely fits this characterization—South Africa's Bobby Locke—is also rated by virtually all of his contemporaries as the greatest putter of all time. When golfers talk of putting, Locke's is generally the first name mentioned, just as Hogan's is when the subject is hitting the ball from tee to green.

Locke would get down behind the ball and study the line for an approximate five seconds, meanwhile laying his putter along the ground at a certain angle, pick up the putter, advance to the ball, assume a slightly closed stance with the clubhead about 2 inches from the ball, take neither more nor less than two practice swings, move up for the actual putt, put the putter in front of the ball, then behind the ball, and stroke. The routine was unvarying. And while I never actually timed the sequence, it seems in retrospect that the cadence was equally unvarying. Also in retrospect, it seems there was little or no variance in the way the ball headed unerringly for the hole.

Billy Casper, who is generally conceded to be one of the best of the modern-day putters, likewise fits my category of pattern putters. He varied his routine a bit more than Locke did—he would sometimes take only a single practice swing and at other times three or four, and the length of time he stood over the ball was not constant—but he moved and acted in a clearly discernible pattern from the time he started lining up the putt until he hit it. And the two had in common that disconcerting (to the opposition) habit of seemingly always rolling the ball right at the hole.

Another pattern putter (as I use the term) is Julius Boros. But he does it all so casually and unobtrusively that his pattern can easily go unnoticed. He does, however, putt with noticeable effectiveness.

I think that the link between pattern putting and good putting is that following a pattern blends the whole operation into a unit. The thing to be avoided, as I see it, is having a marked separation between the preliminaries and the act of starting the clubhead back away from the ball—making the backswing a new and independent movement. This kind of separation leads to what is sometimes insultingly referred to as the lock-up, choke-up, freeze-up putting stroke. In a more charitable and humorous vein, the short but vital putt is called a white-knuckle putt, meaning that the player tenses up to the point of gripping so tightly that the knuckles show white. But in this connection, I have often seen Lloyd Mangrum grip the putter so tight on an important short putt that his knuckles literally would turn white. I do not, however, recall his ever making a bad putt in such a situation.

Strangely, Locke tended to depart from his routine in a crisis situation, as when a single putt could determine the outcome of a major tournament. He has explained to me that, for all his set method, he was essentially a "touch" putter, meaning that he depended on his feel for a putt rather than on any mechanical-type stroke or device for setting things in motion. He said that at times he wished he did have such a device, or artificial aid, so to speak, to use in those situations where his touch seemed to temporarily desert him.

The difference between a touch putter and the other type, as exemplified by Diegel and his outthrust elbows, is a subtle one. One way to put it is that the touch putter will, in a clutch situation, say to himself, "I'll just roll it along the line and into the hole." The other type will think, "I'll give it my patented stroke and it figures to go in." The same-type difference exists also with regard to the full golf swing. On a crisis shot, one player will think simply of taking a good overall swing at the ball. Another will think something like, "I'll start the club back real slow and the rest of it will take care of itself." I guess you could rightly call the latter type the gimmick swingers, and their counterparts on the green would be the gimmick putters. One way the difference sometimes manifests itself is that normally when the gimmick putters miss a short one it is very close; the touch putters seem either to knock it in the hole or miss badly.

In general, putting gimmicks are designed to eliminate—or at least mimimize—the possibility of missing to one particular side of the hole. In Diegel's case, and to a large extent Barber's, the idea was to provide a brace against closing the face of the putter at impact and pulling the ball to the left of the hole. In theory at least, with the left elbow pointing along the intended line, the left wrist can only work like a hinge and cannot roll over so as to turn the face of the putter inward. Thus the miss to the left is theoretically eliminated, provided the player is correctly aligned with his target. So, still going along with the theory of this particular gimmick, the player has blocked off the left side and thus needs only to concentrate on squaring up the putter face at impact so as not to miss to the right. It is quite like Jack Nicklaus's full-shot strategy of making sure that he fades the ball to guarantee against a hook.

Another frequently used gimmick of a different type is to determine in advance not to even watch the ball on its way to the hole—to raise the head and eyes only after the ball has been heard to plop in the hole or has had time to stop rolling. This exercise in self-control can eliminate the not infrequent fault of looking up too soon. But it tends to work to the detriment of such other putting essentials as hitting the ball at the right speed and calculating the break it will take on the way to the hole.

Over the years, golfers have been categorized as "wrist putters" and "arm-and-shoulder putters." These categories are necessarily general rather than specific, since all players use some combination of wrists, arms, and (on long putts) shoulders in striking a putt. The difference is that some players use a short, wristy tap stroke and others a longer, more flowing sweep stroke. The tap putters feel that the short, brisk backswing and forward swing is simpler, less subject to error, more easily timed, and therefore more effective. The sweep putters feel that with the longer stroke the wrist break can be kept to a minimum and that the advantage thereby gained makes theirs the superior method.

Putting authority Billy Casper describes the two basic styles as follows:

> *The wrist method involves primarily the movement of the hands. The arms move very little except*

on long putts, but the hands are quite active because of the hinging action of the wrists.

In the arm-and-shoulder style of putting the wrists are frozen, so to speak, and the basic movement comes from the arms and shoulders. The hands are regarded as being part of the shaft and the wrists are locked firmly in place from start to finish, except for extremely long putts, when the wrists are permitted to break slightly.

(Doubtless for clarity, Casper describes the extremes of the two styles.)

Because of Bobby Jones's enormous success and popularity, the long, flowing sweep style that he used was widely copied during his prime and for some years thereafter. Locke, too, tended to a longer stroke rather than the short tap and, because of his greatness on the greens, exerted a strong influence. Jerry Barber likewise had his share of imitators and has said that "the stroke should be uninhibited in length. Some players prefer the quick jab or 'pop' style on short putts. However, this method is not effective on long putts. Therefore these players must, in effect, develop two putting techniques. I prefer a smooth, unlimited stroke because it works for me on both short and long putts."

One who did develop the two putting techniques and who advocates one technique for short putts and another for long ones is Casper:

On short putts up to 10 or 15 feet, the tap method of putting should be used. The clubhead is swung back in a short arc and the ball is struck rather sharply. The movement of the clubhead is slightly downward and through the ball on the follow-through. This brings the clubhead to a stop 3 or 4 inches past the ball's position at address. On longer putts the hands and arms swing back farther on the backswing and the follow-through is longer.

Barber probably borrowed the term "pop" from Bob Rosburg, a fine player and great putter for many years (and still good enough in 1969 to come within a 4-foot putt of tying for the U.S. Open). "The stroke is a 'pop,'" says Rosburg, making no distinction between short and long putts but speaking only in reference to his own best method. Rosburg regarded Locke as the absolute paragon of putters and noted that Locke was not a "pop" putter by any means.

As for myself, I never actually thought of my own putting stroke in terms of its being a long sweep or a tap, though I'm sure it was more the former. I conceived the putting stroke to be simply a miniature version of the full swing—the putter following the same path on the backswing and forward swing as would the clubhead in the first and last stages of a full swing. I inject this purely personal note here mainly because George Archer, one of the very best putters among the current stars, recently told me that this was the way he conceived his putting stroke.

It becomes clear, then, that length of stroke in putting is largely a matter of individual preference, of feel. Incidentally, the ball will behave no differently whether it is struck with a smooth, sweeping stroke or a brisk tap (or pop). The only factors are the path, speed, and angle of the clubface at impact. Whether smoothly struck or popped, the ball will skid for about a fifth of the overall distance it will travel and then begin rolling. It follows from this, in my opinion at least, that the player should not concern himself with whether the putt will spin or roll but only with its speed and direction. Both science and common logic say that you can't slice or hook a putt. Neither will any particular spin or roll make it fall in the hole more readily—or, by the same token, tend to keep it out of the hole—although for a long time it was widely thought that a ball rolling straight over and over would fall in more readily and that a putt with spin on it would tend to stay out unless it hit the center of the cup.

It is not known at what stage in the development of golf that some player decided it might be effective to use a different grip for putting than for full shots. But somewhere along the line it became common practice among the better putters to place the hands so that the palms directly opposed each other, with the back of the left hand facing the line of the putt. For at least fifty years, the most widely used putting grip has been the one generally known as the reverse overlap. There are many variations of this grip, but its distinguishing characteristic is that the index finger of the left hand does the overlapping. In the regular overlapping grip, of course, it is the little finger of the right hand that overlaps. Hence the term "reverse overlap."

The underlying theory of the reverse overlap is that it gets all of the fingers of the right hand on the shaft, the right hand normally being the dominant hand in striking the putt, the one that supplies most of the touch, feel, sensitivity—or whatever term you choose to apply to the way in which a player judges how hard he should hit the ball to make it cover a given distance. Most good putters say that you should take the clubhead back with the left hand and bring it back through the ball with the right. This fits the facts to a considerable extent and is a point to which the player should give some attention in his practice putting. But in competitive play it is at least highly questionable that he should think in terms of such a distinct separation of the functions of the two hands.

One of the variations of the reverse overlap grip, as exemplified by Arnold Palmer and others, is to extend the left index finger straight down to its full length instead of wrapping it around one of the top two fingers of the right hand. The players who use this variation feel that with the left index finger so positioned it makes a good lever for correctly initiating the backswing.

While the reverse overlap grip, with minor variations, is the most popular, it should be noted that some extremely good putters eschew it in favor of their normal full-shot grip. These include Bobby Locke (regular Vardon overlap) and Bob Rosburg and Art Wall (full finger, nonoverlap grip). This group acts on the theory that using a different grip for putting adds an unnecessary complication to the game.

As far as the P.G.A. tour is concerned, the cross-handed (or reverse-handed) grip was introduced some twenty years ago by Fred Haas, a New Orleans professional and United States Seniors champion in 1965. In recent years it has been used with varying degress of success and permanency by a number of tour players. Among those who found it the most helpful and stuck with it the longest are Johnny Pott, Wes Ellis, Jr., Jim Ferree, British Ryder Cup team member Peter Allis, and, on the Ladies Professional Golfers Association tour, Marilyn Smith. But the cross-handed putting grip got its biggest boost toward popularity from 1969 United States Open champion Orville Moody. Millions saw him, personally or on television, hole some crucial putts in the final stages of that tournament, including the vital short one on the final hole, putting cross-handed. In subsequent interviews, however, Moody said that he used the grip only part of the time, mostly on short putts.

As its name implies, the basic feature of this grip is that the right hand is above the left on the shaft—a sort of left-hander's grip for a right-handed stroke. The grip does, of course, vary in minor details with its different users. The following explanation by Wes Ellis, Jr., covers virtually all of the pertinent points:

> *My grip is the interlocking, with the little finger of my left hand twining around the forefinger of my right hand. This is simply a left-handed interlock as might be used by any left-hander. I putt right-handed, however. The back of my left hand and the palm of my right hand face toward the hole. My thumbs are directly on top of the shaft. Both hands feel the same amount of tension. My hands seem to fit more closely together with the interlock, but I don't think it makes any difference as to the particular kind of grip used so long as it is basically cross-handed. A player simply should experiment until he finds the grip that feels most comfortable for him.*
>
> *The thing that has improved my putting most since I adopted the cross-handed method is the fact that now my*

left hand and wrist remain firm and in control. The right hand never "takes over," causing the left wrist to collapse at impact. The face of the putter remains square to the line for a longer time without any special effort on my part to keep it square. Thus I now feel I have a better chance of putting the ball along the line I select.

The value of a confident attitude in putting has been recognized ever since golf was first played. This aspect of the putting stroke may more properly lie in the field of psychology than of golf-swing analysis. But the player's confidence, or lack of it, does in fact affect the nature of the actual stroke, so a few words on the subject will not be amiss here.

All good putters have been confident putters, and any player's putting skill on a given day is in direct ratio to his confidence on that day. It was Arnold Palmer who brought to full flowering the idea that confidence and determination are valuable adjuncts of the putting stroke. Palmer's whole demeanor on the greens made it clear that he was thinking in terms of how to make the putt and shutting out any thought of missing it. This, I think, is the key to a confident attitude about putting. Few of us can match Palmer's ability to reach a sort of inspirational pitch in a crisis situation. But we can train ourselves to think positively. The process is outlined in *Golf's Winning Stroke: Putting*, written by the editor of this book in cooperation with the editors of *Golf Digest*:

> *The time to begin the mental preparation for putting is the moment your ball gets onto the putting surface. You should then begin to think in terms of making your putt. Note first the general contour of the green as you walk toward it. This can help you judge correctly the direction and degree of break when you actually come to lining up the putt. But more important, observing the green's overall contour starts you off on a constructive train of thought. You begin to think positively. You have the beginning of a resolute attitude.*
> *Then, when you start to line up the putt, concentrate on*

the line the ball must follow to reach the center of the hole. Strive for a mental picture of the ball following the right path and traveling at the speed that will take it into the hole just as it loses its last bit of momentum.

You can train yourself in this sort of thinking. By doing so you can shut out the negative thoughts that rob so many golfers of whatever chance they might have to become good putters. If you are busy figuring out ways to make a putt, you can't be thinking of ways to miss it.

Since you have a choice in this respect—either to think positively or negatively about making the putt—do not start to imagine everything that could possibly go wrong. Don't say to yourself, "I must be careful not to be short and also I must guard against hitting the ball too hard." And don't say, "I mustn't underplay the break or overplay it."

Moreover, don't let your mind wander ahead to the situation you will be in if you miss the putt. Stick to the business at hand, which is making your putt drop.

If, for instance, you hit a particularly nice shot onto the green and have a good chance for a birdie, don't start telling yourself what a shame it would be to fail to capitalize on so great an opportunity.

Similarly, if an opponent holes a long putt, and you find yourself with a short putt for a tie instead of the win you had expected, don't let it throw you.

Neither of the above situations will disturb you, or at least they will be far less likely to, if you just maintain your positive train of thought.

A further point that the golfer should not lose sight of is that even a "perfectly" struck putt will not always go in. This knowledge can help him overcome the frustration of seeing two or three of his best putts miss the hole just as he thought they were about to drop—an experience that can cause him to alter his putting stroke to its detriment. The team of British scientists referred to earlier constructed a machine to strike putts very consistently on a chosen line and at a predetermined speed. The machine was then tested against a team of professional golfers. From 6 feet the machine made 98 percent of putts as compared with 55 percent for the pros. From

20 feet the machine missed half the time and the pros almost 9 out of 10 times. At 60 feet the machine missed 80 times per 100 tries and the pros 97 times per 100. The obvious conclusion is that to make a sizable putt the player must not only strike the ball precisely but also have a little luck.

Present-day golf has produced no putters whom I would consider markedly superior to such greats of the recent past as Bobby Locke, Paul Runyan, Johnny Revolta, Walter Hagen, Bobby Jones, and several others. Today, however, there are many more good-to-excellent putters than there were a couple of decades or so ago. Time was when a player could do reasonably well on the tournament circuit—and even win an occasional tournament—while putting just fairly well. Nowadays there are so many good hitters competing that to win a tournament—or even place near the top—the player must putt somewhere between good and sensational. This is why practice putting greens at tournament sites are busy places.

Other golfers besides myself, notably Gary Player, have emphasized the salubrious effect of good putting on the swings that produce the other shots. It is a remarkable thing how a couple of good putts early in the round will smooth out a player's swing. Conversely, a couple of missed short putts can have a plainly adverse effect on the player's swing from tee to green. It is a matter of confidence, which good putting breeds and bad putting stifles.

In connection with the mental aspects of putting, it will help some players produce a better putting stroke if they realize that the time consumed in making it is about half a second, or half the time consumed in hitting a full shot. And, as is the case on full shots, the player is totally committed once the forward swing is started. That is to say, there is not sufficient time to make any corrective movements or adjustments after the backswing is completed. This means that the player should fully program his putt before he starts the stroke, that he should decide firmly and finally on line, speed, and the rest of it before initiating the backswing. This will help avoid the timid, indecisive stroke that causes so many missed putts. The point is that if the player realizes he can't make effective adjustments during the actual stroke, he will be less inclined to try.

It goes without saying, the player should try to find a putter in which he has full confidence. Some players will undoubtedly be helped by getting one of the recently developed putters in which the head weight is more evenly distributed by means of shifting more weight toward the heel and toe of the club. This reduces the necessity for striking the ball squarely in the center of the clubface. It enlarges the "sweet-spot" and increases the margin for error.

Some Special Swings

In developing a golf swing designed to hit the ball at least reasonably straight and in a trajectory conducive to maximum distance, golfers have also developed a repertoire of swings designed to make the ball curve markedly left or right in flight or fly extraordinarily low or high, depending on the circumstances. These are usually called "trouble" shots. Even the most consistently straight hitters must have a working knowledge and some mastery of such shots. Anybody who hits the ball far enough to be a potential low-handicap player will on occasion find his normal flight path to the green blocked by trees or some other obstacle that he must go around, over, or under. Putting it another way, the expert golfer must know how to slice the ball, hook it, hit it low, hit it high, and do some of these things in combination—high slices, low hooks, and so on. The necessity for hitting such shots arises, of course, from the fact that no golfer with any appreciable power always has an open shot to the green. This is simply a fact of golf life. All golfers will occasionally find themselves in positions near the green when a routine golf shot —one that rises to normal height and lands on the green with an ordinary amount of backspin—will not do the required job. In short, there is more to expert golf than meets the non-expert eye.

There is no point in saying that one particular golfer, past or present, exemplifies the trouble-shot technique to the extent that his methods can be presented as embodying all there is to be learned about this phase of the game. Arnold Palmer, who has been known to stray from the fairway enough to give himself a number of opportunities to play "recovery" shots, is certainly one of the more imaginative and effective players of trouble shots; Ben Hogan, who was so rarely off line that it is hard to conceive of him having to recover, also was a master of all the unusual shots to be described in this section—plus possibly a few that somehow eluded me. It is generally the bold, aggressive players (like Palmer) who hit the most spectacular recovery shots, as they refuse to play it safe. The situations that call for a hook or slice to reach the green, for example, also present the possibility of a short, safe shot back onto the fairway. And it is part of being a truly good trouble-shot player to be able to assess the possible punishments against the possible rewards and judge accordingly the type of shot to try.

For most golfers, the simplest trouble shot is the deliberate slice. In fact, if an habitual slicer needs to curve the ball around an intervening obstacle he can just hit the ball with his normal swing and get the desired results. It helps, however, to understand the principles involved. The ball slices because the clubhead is brought into the ball in such a way as to impart a left-to-right spin. This can be done in two basic ways. One is to bring the clubhead across the ball from right to left (from outside the line to inside the line) . The other is to have the clubface open (angled to the right) at impact. Used in combination, these two techniques will produce a real roundhouse slice.

In general, if the single technique of cutting across the ball is used, the ball will take off to the left and begin slicing when some of its original momentum is lost and the sidespin begins taking effect. The reason the ball starts off to the left is that this is the direction in which the clubhead is traveling at impact. If the clubhead comes into the ball along a straight line toward the target but is angled to the right, the resultant movement of the ball to the right will be almost immediate and gradual in contrast to the sharp curve brought about by the cut-across, outside-in swing. The theory here is that the ball leaves the clubface in the general direction in which the clubhead is traveling and changes course as a result of side-spin. (The angle of the clubhead at impact also influences the direction in which the ball takes off, but to a lesser extent than does the line on which the clubhead is moving.)

These considerations are important in judging the type of shot you want to try to play. To illustrate the point, let's assume that there is a tree some 50 yards in front of you blocking your straight path to the green. You want to start the ball off to the left and have it curve sharply back to the right after passing the tree. In this situation, the emphasis should be on cutting across the ball. The other method is liable to start the ball moving right too soon, before passing the intervening tree. In another situation you might want a more gradual slice, which in current golf terminology is called an "exaggerated fade."

There are a number of adjustments in overall technique calculated to produce a slice. First, you can "weaken" your grip by merely turning both hands over to the left. If your normal grip finds the V's formed by the thumb and fore-finger of each hand pointing to the right eye, make them point to the left eye. This adjustment promotes having the clubface open at impact, because it makes it harder to square the clubface up as you come into the ball. Naturally, this adjustment fits the pattern for the more gradual type of slice described above.

Second, you can adjust your stance to make it more open. Assuming a square stance, advance the right foot a few inches toward the line. With this stance, the right hip tends to block the passage of the arms into the hitting area, so the plane of the swing is moved outward and the clubhead is brought into the ball from outside the line (the cut-across). This adjustment best fits the pattern for a sharply curving slice.

As an aid to producing the outside-in swing, start the club-head back outside the line. This will move the right elbow out and away from the body, which is a feature of the out-side-in swing.

Clubs with the least amount of face loft can be made to produce the sharpest slices. To go slightly into the physics of it, the less backspin the ball has on it, the more sidespin it can have, and the least-lofted clubs produce the least back-spin, as may be seen if you imagine hitting the ball a level blow with a club of no loft at all. Actually, backspin and side-spin both work to produce a curve in the flight of the ball. The backspin works to make the ball curve upward, an effect that gravity works to counteract.

For a more practical approach, a good man to heed is trick-shot artist Paul Hahn, who has to understand the use of spin to work out some of the shots in his repertoire.

If you think about it, you will realize and understand that the less lofted the clubface, the sharper slice you can produce. What you want is maximum left-to-right spin. With the more-lofted clubs, you get a lot of underspin, which to some extent counteracts the left-to-right spin. Hence the sharpest, biggest slices can be produced with the two least-lofted clubs in your bag. They are, of course, the driver and the putter. But getting the ball airborne with either of these clubs is difficult unless the lie is exceptionally good, and it is not advocated that either should be used for deliberate slicing except in rare circum-

stances. These circumstances would be that a very sharp slice was needed, and that the lie was sufficiently good to eliminate the problem of getting the ball airborne so as to enable the sidespin to take effect.

Under these conditions, the driver might be used if a long slice was needed, and, more rarely, the putter might be used if the distance was short and a low, quick-breaking slice was the only solution. In both instances, you would open the clubface, which naturally and automatically increases the loft of the club. The idea behind using either the driver or the putter for a slice shot is that in opening the clubface you get extra sidespin.

Let me cite a couple of instances in which the driver or putter might be used. First, the driver: Say that the ball was directly behind a tree whose branches extended down to a point only 6 feet or so above the ground. Say that the lie was fluffy, with the ball resting on top of the grass sufficiently to allow you to get the clubface on the ball and get it airborne, and the distance needed was about 175 yards or more. With a more-lofted club, you might get the ball up so quickly that it would hit the lower limbs. Also, you might not get a sharp enough slice with this more-lofted club. So you take the driver, open the clubface a bit, concentrate on contacting the underside of the ball, and swing away. The result would figure to be a shot that got some 4 feet off the ground, traveled straight for some 10 to 20 yards, and then, as the left-to-right spin took effect, curved nicely back to the right.

The extreme conditions that would bring about the use of the putter would roughly duplicate those described above, except that the shot would be 50 to 75 yards or so shorter.

These two shots, admittedly, approach the realm of trick shots, and are not prescribed for use in less than fairly expert hands. The real purpose in describing them is to illustrate the point that straight-faced clubs are best for deliberate slices. For the great majority of players, the 2-iron and the 2-wood are best for deliberate slicing. If the shot needed is fairly short one, merely choke down on the 2-iron and take a half to three-quarter swing.

The hook, like the slice, is the result of striking the ball an oblique blow with the clubface, causing it to move across the face of the club during impact and making the front of the ball spin right to left in flight (for the hook). A ball will always tend to curve in its flight through the air if it is spinning upon its own axis, and, unless other forces intervene, it will curve in whatever direction its front surface is spinning.

For all practical purposes, what has been said about the intentional slice can simply be reversed and applied to the intentional hook. Make the grip stronger by turning both hands over to the right to promote a quicker closing of the clubface. Close the stance to promote a more inside-out swing. Take the clubhead back inside the line to facilitate bringing it back into the ball along this same path.

To be an effective user of the intentional slice and hook, some marked differences in the performances of the two shots should be recognized. Neither the slice nor the hook will cover as much distance in the air as a straight shot hit with equal power. A ball spinning on a horizontal axis, as it does when hit straight (a square blow instead of an oblique one), will stay airborne longer and fly farther. A hooking ball, however, will roll farther than a straight-hit one and may well travel farther overall, especially if the ground it lands on is hard and conducive to roll. Conversely, the sliced ball tends to roll less than one hit straight. This stems from the nature of the spin and has a scientific explanation, but it is enough for the golfer simply to know the facts and take them into account. Also, as every golfer knows, the slice tends to soar and the hook to duck down. For this explanation, we will borrow from our friends the British golf scientists.

By and large, hooked shots tend to fly low, sometimes extremely low, and run when they hit the ground, whereas slices tend to fly high and stop quickly when they pitch (fall to the ground).

Why should this be? The answer lies in the asymmetry of the golf swing and so, of the club. The shaft comes into the head at about 55 degrees from the horizontal as it lies upon the ground, and the golfer swings the clubhead through a plane inclined at anything from 45 degrees to 60 degrees.

Turning the face of the club to the right thus, in effect, increases its loft (try it) and consequently both the height at which it sends the ball off and at the same time the amount of backspin it gives it. It doesn't take a great deal of this effect to produce the characteristically soaring flight we associate with a full-blooded slice.

Exactly the reverse applies to the hook. Turning the face to the left reduces the effective loft, and thus starts the ball off lower and with reduced backspin.

This, of course, is why the expert player aiming to play a fade will often "hood" the face of the club by standing a bit ahead of the normal stance position and then carrying his hands through well ahead of the clubhead as it strikes the ball. This effectively keeps the loft down to normal, despite having the clubface slightly open to the line of his swing.

It is correspondingly why, when aiming to play a big high hook around a tree, the expert will be very likely to play the ball more forward in his stance than usual and whip the head through ahead of the hands, so far as the lie permits. By so doing he maintains or even increases the effective loft, despite the turning of the clubface to the left. If he does not do something like this, the aiming of the face to the left of the line of his swing will tend to produce a ducking flight instead of the trajectory he needs.

So far, we have dealt with the intentional slice and hook as they pertain to curving the ball around obstacles. There is another use of these shots that is considerably less-known but which in given circumstances can be highly effective. The best way to describe this use is by example. Say that your ball comes to rest a few feet to the right of a tree—too close for you to take a normal stance and backswing for a full straight shot. So you test these stance-and-backswing conditions on the basis of hitting an intentional slice. To stand as if to start the ball off to the left and slice it back in, you will want to move your feet back by maybe 8 to 12 inches. This may give you the room you need to take your stance. Also, for the slice, you will want to take the club back outside the line. This may give you the needed room to take a full backswing.

It is possible, of course, that the conditions of the shot may be worse for trying a slice than for hitting the ball straight. You may need to move the feet forward from where your normal stance would be instead of back. And a backswing inside the line may be your best bet for avoiding interference from overhanging limbs. In that case, test the conditions on the basis of hitting an intentional hook. The key is that you can vary your stance and backswing considerably as between setting up to hit a slice, a straight ball, or a hook. The fact that you are blocked off from using one technique does not necessarily mean you are blocked off from using another. It takes a bit of imagination, plus trying all available methods, before deciding that you don't have a shot at the green.

In any given situation, after you have considered the use of the intentional slice or hook individually and have not found a solution, think of the high slice and the low slice, the high hook and the low hook. We have seen that the low shot goes naturally with the hook and the high shot with the slice, but it has also been shown that low slices and high hooks, while slightly more difficult to bring off, are quite possible.

Something of the technique of hitting an extra-high or low shot as needed is revealed in the discussion of hitting intentional slices and hooks. The open clubface, to add loft, is a key to hitting the type of shot often needed to clear an intervening tree; and the closed clubface, which reduces loft, is part of hitting a low skimmer designed to fly under the limbs of a tree.

Two things principally are needed to produce a sharply rising high shot. One is that the leading edge of the opened clubface should make initial contact with the underside of the ball, to the extent that the lie makes this possible. The other prime ingredient is that the clubhead should be moved through and under the ball, maintaining the open position. If the ball is setting well upon the grass, with a good cushion underneath it, the clubhead can be maneuvered so that it is beginning to move upward at impact.

To set up this type of shot, position the ball well forward, opposite the toe of the left foot or just inside it. The purpose of this positioning is to make contact as the clubhead reaches the very end of its descent arc, or, assuming an especially cushiony lie and the need for a shot of the steepest possible trajectory, as the clubhead begins to move upward. Do not, however, overdo the business of trying to hit the ball on the upswing. This can lead to getting the clubhead too far ahead of the hands at impact, which can in turn lead to a shank.

For the low shot, you generally reverse the high-shot pattern. Toe the clubface in a bit to shut off some of its natural loft, position the ball well back in the stance, keep the hands well ahead of the clubhead as you move through the ball, and be sure the club is still in its descent arc at impact.

Miniswings

In recent years, professional-tournament performances have been studied and analyzed from almost every conceivable angle—length of drives, percentage of greens hit in the regulation number of strokes, average distance from the pin on iron shots from various distances, number of putts per round, and so on. From this welter of information it has been figured that the professionals on the P.G.A. tour play an average of some eight short-approach shots (70 yards or less) per 18 holes. This means that on an average day they have ten putts for birdies and eight to save pars (throwing out the relatively rare instances of putts for eagles and, at the other end of the scale, the times the first putt is for a bogey or worse).

Analyzing the information still further and adding a few touches of estimation and guesswork, some experts have figured that a professional could, by improving his short game (chipping and pitching) "appreciably," cut two strokes a round off his average 18-hole score. There are probably at least fifty professionals to whom such an improvement would mean more than $100,000 per year in additional prize money. But for most tour players, improving their short game to this extent would be quite unlikely, considering that nearly all of them are already very good at it and that they can only spread their practice time between the various phases of the game so much. But the question of how much the average golfer could improve his score by better chipping and pitching is another question. No doubt he gets more shots per round within the 70-yard-and-under range than the pro, and hence more chances to save strokes by getting on and down in two shots. But then, he does not figure to be as good a putter as the pro and probably wouldn't capitalize on as many good short shots by one-putting. And, of course, the average golfer's available practice time is far more limited than the pro's and should be spread among the game's various phases.

The question is confusing, but I think there are at least a couple of clear conclusions to be drawn from it. One is that the average golfer could benefit greatly through an improved short game. Another is that he could progress along this line more rapidly if he knew and used the basic tactics that are common practice on today's tournament circuit.

As with trouble shots, no single player stands out as the best in this particular field—none whose technique around the greens clearly suggests itself as a model. The fact is that all the consistent money-winners necessarily have good short games, and it is in the nature of this phase of golf, with its reliance on the elusive qualities of "touch" and "feel," that a given player will be a master of it one day and maybe no better than mediocre the next. There are, however, some players who have impressed me as having especially sound techniques around the greens. From my early days on the tour I think naturally of Johnny Revolta, a wizard if ever there was one.

Of the current players, Billy Maxwell and Deane Beman are among the very best at getting down in two from near the green. Maxwell and Beman are relatively short hitters, as was Revolta in his prime, and they had to excel at the short game to beat the longer hitters. Of the topflight strikers of the ball who also approach genius around the greens, Billy Casper stands out, as does Gene Littler. The basics to be presented in this section comprise something of each of their methods, which are so nearly alike that you really can't say that the one handles a given situation any better than the other.

Actually, the swing that any fine player uses for less-than-full shots is neither more nor less than a shortened version of his full swing. Naturally, in discussing this phase of the game, you don't get into the business of turning the shoulders and hips. In the shortened version of the swing, these matters take care of themselves. It is important to avoid starting the downswing with the hands (hitting from the top), but when getting maximum power into the swing is not a factor, this fault can easily be avoided.

The shortened swing does present one problem that is absent, or virtually so, in the full swing. On a full shot, the player normally selects a club with which he figures to cover the needed distance and hits the ball almost as hard as he can. On the less-than-full shots the question of just how much power to apply is more involved. The player is capable of knocking the ball too far as well as leaving it short, neither of which is much of a problem on the full shot if the right club is chosen and the swing is sound. In short, there is more judgment involved in the short shot than the full one.

All this points up the need for programming the shot fully and decisively before starting the swing. The player should strive for a clear mental picture of the projected flight of the ball, where he wants it to land, and the bounce and roll he can logically anticipate. Lacking this firm plan, he is subject to having misgivings while in the act of making the stroke. It may strike him in midstroke that he should add more power to the swing to avoid being short, or he may let up on the swing for fear of going over. In either case he will wreck the needed rhythm of the swing, making it sloppy or jerky when smoothness is what he needs. Even a cursory study of the short-game techniques, of say, Casper or Maxwell or Beman will show the distinct separation between planning and execution.

In modern golf terminology, the term "pitch" shot refers to a high, soft, lob-type shot that rolls only a short distance after landing on the green. The club generally used for it is the pitching wedge, although a 9-iron or an 8-iron might be used if the shot is to be played into a brisk wind. The observant golfer will note that wind direction affects the flight characteristics of a shot. A wind blowing toward you will not only cut down the distance the ball flies through the air but will increase the effect of backspin and thereby decrease the roll. For example, a shot hit with an 8-iron into a 20-mile-an-hour wind will perform almost exactly like a shot hit with a pitching wedge when the wind factor is negligible. You will not see the experts use a wedge for a shot into a strong wind unless the conditions of the shot demand an absolute minimum of roll. The high, soft flight normally produced by a wedge lays the ball liable to being buffeted about in the wind, making it hard to assess both direction and distance.

As was implied in the statement that the same principles apply to the short and full swings, the swing for the pitch should be smoothly back in the plane and smoothly down and through the ball. Any motion of the hands designed to help lift the ball must be avoided. If extra height and backspin is desired, open the clubface a bit and concentrate on making initial contact with the underside of the ball.

On the pitch shot especially, it will be helpful to know something about the interaction of the clubface and the ball during the fraction of a second the two are in contact. At first the ball begins sliding upward on the angled clubface. Then the dimples on the ball and the grooves of the clubface act together to make the ball start rolling (spinning). At the instant the slide turns fully into roll, say the scientists, the ball takes its maximum backspin. This may mean little or nothing to the nonscientific golfer, but it does show the folly of trying to impart loft or backspin with a lifting motion of the hands just before or during impact.

The chip shot—to make a sort of arbitrary distinction—is normally played from just off the green, has a lower trajectory than the pitch, and is usually planned to land a few feet on the green and roll the rest of the way to the hole. As this indicates, it can be played with any of the iron clubs from the wedge up to and even including the 2-iron, although the experts tend to limit the choice of clubs for chipping to those ranging upward in number and loft from the 5-iron. The swing for the chip shot is, of course, quite short—much like the swing for a long putt, except that the forward swing is more sharply downward and through the ball.

The very essence of effective chipping is exact planning. The stroke required for the execution of the shot is well within the capabilities of all golfers. Only if the player abruptly changes the tempo of his swing or moves his head enough to get the stroke out of its short and simple groove is he apt to flub the shot. And both these errors can normally be avoided if the player first decides how he means to play the shot and then, with this decision firmly settled on, goes about the business of making the stroke.

Taking it step by step, in the routine favored by all the experts I've observed, it goes like this:

1. Get a full and definite mental picture of the intended shot—its trajectory, the spot on which it should land, the bounces and roll it should take to reach the hole as it runs out of momentum.
2. Choose a club with the loft to fit this chosen pattern.
3. Execute the stroke.

The choice of the club is based directly on the shot-pattern chosen. A single illustration should cover both points. Say that the ball lies 15 feet off the putting surface on a level lie.

The pin is 40 feet past the edge of the green, with generally level ground intervening. The green is moderately soft and of medium speed. So you picture that with the normal loft of a 6-iron you can chip the ball to a spot 10 feet past the front edge of the green, and with the normal trajectory and back-spin that a 6-iron produces, the bounces and roll will take the ball the remaining 30 feet.

I have postulated a basic chip shot. There are literally end-less variations of it. The green may slope upward toward you or downward away from you, which will affect the amount of roll to be expected. If we vary the example cited above to say that you are hitting into an upslope, you would want to take maybe a 5-iron instead of a 6 and toe the club in a bit to decrease the effective loft and thereby get a lower trajectory and more roll. With the green sloping away from you a more-lofted club would be indicated, maybe a 9-iron or a wedge. It would be impossible to describe all the variations of the shot. The point is that all the conditions of the shot must be taken into account.

In suggesting that you select a landing target some 10 feet past the edge of the green, the idea is that you want to insure that the ball hits safely on the putting surface. You want some margin for error. If you try to land the ball just a foot or so past the edge, a slight error in execution may make the ball hit a foot or two short in the normally higher grass and rougher terrain surrounding the green. You would then get considerably less roll than you calculated and maybe an erratic bounce. You would be taking a needless chance. In this con-nection, if you are uncertain as to which club to chip with, pick the more lofted one. You'll feel safer with it and be less likely to come up with the timorous, hesitant stroke that causes so many flubbed chip shots.

Swinging
the Right Club

It might appear that selecting a club for a given shot is totally separate from the golf swing itself, but there is a connection. If the player is confident that he has the right club in his hands when he steps up to the ball and goes through the motions preliminary to swinging, that confidence will be reflected in the swing that follows. That is to say, the swing is apt to be one of the player's better ones— smooth, unhurried, effective. Conversely, if the player starts his swing still thinking that he may have too little or too much club for the distance needed, that uncertainty will also be reflected in his swing.

If the fear is that he doesn't have enough club, he will almost certainly try to compensate by throwing in some extra-distance-producing effort, an almost sure way to wreck one's timing. The uneasy feeling of maybe having too much club is almost equally a swing-wrecker, but golfers generally tend to underclub far more often than overclub.

Actually, in themselves, the faults of underclubbing and overclubbing are relatively minor. If, for instance, the player took a normal swing with a 6-iron on a shot for which a 5-iron was the right club, he would figure merely to come up 10 to 20 yards short but still in line with his target. Similarly, with one club too much but no change in the normal swing, the ball would figure to go past by the distance indicated above. In neither case might the error be serious, particularly if the shot was to a big green. The main trouble, then, lies not so much in the club-choice error per se as in the player's uncertainty, as manifested in his execution of the shot. Thus it follows that the player's swing can in fact be improved through acquiring a sound basis for club selection.

The best information on the subject comes from the good players past and present. I feel it safe to say that there was never a great player who was not also a wise and precise club-selector. It is something of a marvel that the better players on today's P.G.A. tour can come to a golf course for the first time and, after a couple of practice rounds, know its distances better than many of its veteran members do. Many of the playing professionals, of course, chart a golf course the first time around it. They choose a check point in what they call the landing area for a normal drive and pace off the yardage from there to the green. Afterward, they can pace off the distance back to or up to where their drive is, add or subtract yardage as indicated, and know how far it is to the green. Many of them—Jack Nicklaus, Dave Hill, R. H. Sikes, and others—carry a scorecard or notebook in which to note these distances for daily reference while the tournament is going on. But many others do not—knowing that wind and other atmospheric conditions make distances strictly relative from a golf standpoint—and prefer to choose a club on the basis of how the shot looks to them at the time it is to be made. Charting a golf course in writing is, in fact, a relatively new practice. It was Jack Nicklaus who popularized it.

Nevertheless, good golfers have much in common in the way they go about choosing a club for a shot. There has long existed what amounts to a basic system. Probably the best way to describe the basis of the system is to describe what it assuredly is not. The good players do not—as so many bad players do—look at a given shot and choose for its execution the most-lofted club with which they can possibly reach the green, swinging with all their might and counting on an absolutely solid hit. This, to their great detriment, is the basis used by many players who, as the British say, play at long handicaps. Using such a basis is in itself a handicap and to a considerable extent accounts for the fact that many young players who hit the ball long and well fail to score anywhere near their potential. For some invalid reason, young players in particular seem to feel that it is somehow better to reach a green with, say, a 7-iron than a 6-iron.

The true basis is that the right club is one with which the objective can be reached comfortably, without strain—one that will produce the needed distance, or safely near it, even though the shot may be hit a small fraction off center (only a few shots per round are hit absolutely solid, even by the best players).

The dominant thought in the good player's mind is that he must have a club that will comfortably produce the distance he needs. I use the term "comfortably" in this connection in the same sense that most professionals do—to mean a club that will allow the player to put out of his mind any need for straining to reach the green, thus allowing him freedom of mind to concentrate on making a good, sound swing.

We have so far dealt mainly with the problems inherent in taking too little club. It is also quite possible, of course, to overestimate the distance and take too much club. Of the two problems, however, that of underclubbing is so much more prevalent that the one of overclubbing can be handled more briefly. One of the reasons that the average player takes too much club is that he gets so fed up with taking too little club and falling short that he overcompensates. Another is that he goes too much by the club he normally hits from a given position and fails to take into account certain factors that call for less club than usual—more of a following wind, less of an adverse wind, lighter than normal atmosphere, and the like.

The obvious moral of the above is that each shot should be judged, from a club-selection standpoint, on the conditions that prevail at the moment it is to be hit. Prior experience is a constant factor, to be sure, but the player must be flexible and able to adapt. This is a knack that the playing pros—who see a different course with different topographical and atmospheric conditions almost every week—must develop in order to survive. Also, the pros develop a knack for shunting aside any will-puzzling worry about having the wrong club. They are able to separate the choice of the club from the execution of the shot. Call it a fatalistic attitude—they tell themselves that they may have picked the wrong club but are not going to compound the error by making a sloppy or jerky swing on top of it.

The player who tends to make bad club choices, or who continually questions his own decisions in this matter, should go to a practice range and run a thorough test on himself and his clubs. He should hit a representative number of shots with each club, paying particular attention to the true distance he gets with a normal (for him) shot. Such a test can make him both a more competent and more confident judge of the club to use in a given situation—and competence and confidence are mutually valuable in club selection.

The club-selector must always be on guard against being unduly influenced by the selection of another player. I have very often seen players take a wrong club because they overheard a scrap of conversation from another player. "Looks like a 6 to me," some player in the group may say to his partner or caddy, or even to himself. Meanwhile, ol' rabbit-ears has been fiddling with the 4-iron for a shot of roughly the same distance. But now he decides that a 4-iron is too much club. He takes a 5 or a 6, leaps at the ball in a misguided effort to get extra power, and . . . well, the rest of the story is obvious. It also has a moral: Use your own best judgment. You alone know how you intend to hit the ball, what the lie is like, and so on. Furthermore, the other guy may be grossly underestimating the distance.

To sum up: Take a club in which you have full confidence. Be sure you have enough club, but don't overdo the point. Train yourself so that when you choose a club you put all doubts out of your mind and can give your full attention to executing the shot. It is also wise to consider whether the worst trouble is over the green or short of it and to choose your club accordingly.

Your Swing

No matter how thoroughly you understand the overall theory of the golf swing, or how intelligently selective you may be in choosing from among all the opinions offered, there remains the problem of developing a swing that is distinctively your own—one that you are familiar with both as to its capabilities and its limitations. You should develop a repeating swing. Even a flawed swing can be effective in terms of scoring (which is what the game is about), provided it can consistently produce the same results time after time. The example that comes to mind is Bobby Locke, who took the club back inside the line much too sharply and quickly to suit the game's purists and hooked virtually every full shot he hit, yet was for a number of years one of the half-dozen best players in the world. This is not to say that you should ignore the precepts and examples of such fundamentally sound swingers as Bobby Jones, Ben Hogan, Sam Snead, Arnold Palmer, Jack Nicklaus, or others I could mention. It is to say that one effective golf swing can differ from another in a number of minor details.

The way to build your swing is through intelligent practice. If this suggests that not all golf practice is intelligent—or even helpful—then I have made my point, which is to lead into a discussion of how theory can best be applied to practice ("practice" here having a double meaning).

I shall emphasize at the outset that successful professionals long ago learned that experimentation must be carried out on the practice range or during practice rounds and not in actual competition. When you begin a competitive round, exorcise from your mind the theoretical concepts and the gimmicks and resolve simply to hit the ball as well as you can while at the same time using the best strategy of which you are capable. This point is most important, which is why I have placed it ahead of some more elementary phases of learning through practice.

I think the most elementary thing about practice is that every part of it should have a definite purpose. Every practice shot should be aimed at a specific target, even though the practicing player should be thinking basically in terms of causes rather than results. After each shot, the player should pause long enough to analyze what happened and why, regardless of whether the shot was good or bad. It is just as valuable to give thought to what is being done right as it is to what is being done wrong—perhaps even more so. There is a tendency among golfers to accept good shots without question and to analyze the swing only when something goes wrong. It is a tendency that should be resisted.

Here I want to pass along a suggestion from Ben Hogan, who probably is golf's most astute practicer as well as its most astute player. Hogan said he liked to carry a small notebook with him when he went out to practice and jot down just what phase of his swing he was working on and what progress he was making. Then, at the beginning of his next practice session, he would consult his notes from the previous one to determine his starting point. He thus gave his practice program a continuity often lacking even among the very best players.

Hogan's custom would be especially valuable to the average amateur who, unlike Hogan, can rarely practice on a daily schedule, and who, also unlike Hogan, might tend to forget the experience of his last session. This presupposes, of course, that the player is dedicated to the improvement of his golf game to the extent that he wants to extract the maximum benefit from his practices. I would scarcely expect every golfer to be so dedicated, but anyone serious enough about his game to go to the practice tee in the first place should at least bear in mind the need for a certain amount of self-analysis between swings. The player who just goes out and thoughtlessly hits one ball after another is not really practicing at all, merely exercising.

One valuable practice aid is to relate each shot to some actual situation on the golf course. If you are practicing with the driver, for instance, imagine that you are driving from the tee of a particular hole with which you are familiar and try to fit the drive to the conditions of that hole. Start with the first hole on your home course, for example, and proceed through the drives you will need on each succeeding hole that calls for a driver off the tee.

I'm sure that a great many golfers do not realize that some valuable practice can be carried on in any area big enough to allow a full swing of the club—your backyard, for instance. Just practicing the grip can be surprisingly beneficial—even though not too much of a thrill. The idea here takes in both getting a basically correct grip and becoming thoroughly familiar with the feel of it. Far more shots than most golfers might believe are mis-hit or hit off line because of inconsistent gripping. In actual play, gripping the club tends to be an automatic thing, the player taking it for granted that he is not varying his grip from shot to shot. But the fact is that it is quite easy to vary the grip slightly without being aware of it, and just a slight variance can make a vast difference in how the shot comes off. Hence the player who is familiar enough with his own grip to detect slight changes in it through feel is at a distinct advantage.

Another valuable practice tactic is to work on the backswing alone or in conjunction with the waggle. The twin objectives are to go smoothly into the backswing and to stay in the correct plane so that as nearly as possible the player always hits the same slot at the top of the backswing. It will be helpful to follow the backswing exercise by practicing the initial downswing movement. Simply start the hips moving laterally and back around to the left—nothing more. The twin objectives here are to get the feel of moving the body correctly and in advance of the arms and hands, and to get it clearly in mind that the hip movement automatically lowers the hands to just above hip level and starts the shoulders moving. In carrying out this exercise, remember that this is the last movement of the swing that can be consciously directed. The rest of it will be automatic and will be correct or otherwise depending on the correctness or incorrectness of what has occurred up to that point.

Practicing the separate movements individually will help to make them more nearly automatic—the product of what Hogan and others have called "muscle memory." Bear in mind that the more movements of the swing you can automatically carry out correctly the better off you are. You may, like Palmer, be able to concentrate solely on keeping the head still, meanwhile being secure in the knowledge that the rest of it will work as programmed. Or, perhaps even more ideally, you may, like Hogan, make the mechanics of the swing so nearly automatic that your only conscious thought will be to "knock the damn ball in the hole."

I can factually state on the basis of personal experience that practicing the full swing with no ball there to hit can be at least as valuable as actually hitting practice shots. What this does is facilitate a free release through the hitting segment of the swing. Bobby Jones called it "free-wheeling through impact," which he said was the feeling he got when he was playing his best. In the search for the perfect golf swing, British golf scientists later confirmed the rightness of this feeling:

> Bobby Jones's feeling of "free-wheeling" through impact suggests that he was one of the few golfers who instinctively realized this, and that he succeeded in discharging all of his effort into the clubhead before he came into impact, then left the clubhead to get on with the stroke on its own. Which is what it is going to do anyway, whatever any player may feel or think.
> In a golf swing, there are thus two entirely separate actions. The golfer himself just gets the clubhead swinging as fast and as truly as he can before impact, and then can affect the stroke no more. The clubhead, travelling at the speed and direction already given to it by the player's swing, then hits the ball on its own, according to the laws governing its movement as a free body.

If you are wondering why the presence of the ball there to be hit inhibits this feeling of free release, or free-wheeling, through impact, I would have to say that I don't know exactly. I do know, as do all golfers, that just about every practice swing a player makes is a better swing than he makes to actually hit the ball. What is indicated, then, is a way to learn to hit the ball with a swing as nearly identical as possible to the player's practice swing. I think the way may well be to practice the full swing until it becomes the natural way to swing at the ball. It is the muscle-memory thing again.

I am fully aware that practicing the swing is not as interesting or satisfying as actually hitting the ball. By the same token, practicing the separate movements individually is even more demanding of patience and dedication than practicing the full swing. Much of the pleasure of golf derives from sensing that solid impact between clubhead and ball and, as Palmer said in one of his more poetic moods, seeing that white ball in flight arched against the blue of the sky.

No doubt about that. But you can look at it from the standpoint that any drudgery you undergo in improving the swing will pay for itself by increasing the frequency with which you hit the kind of shots that arch against the sky and all that. So it all works out to profit.

Model Swinger Gene Littler

Among the great players of the present, I believe the one whose style could be studied most profitably is Gene Littler. This is not to say that Littler is necessarily the best swinger on the P.G.A. circuit—although I think that any expert would place him very high on any list of the best swingers the game has known. But the reason I would suggest him as a model is that Gene makes the correct moves in a golf swing so readily apparent. He is what could be called a textbook swinger—the possessor of a textbook swing that covers all the points clearly, completely, concisely, and, so to speak, in simple "language" easily understandable to the layman.

First of all, Gene illustrates the point that the player should begin to settle into his own correct tempo from the time he starts to approach the ball for the shot. He is all smoothness and rhythm as he approaches the ball, takes his usual two practice swings, and moves in to take his stance.

Here, and on the following eleven pages, Gene Littler demonstrates his near-perfect swing with the iron.

He is completely unhurried but not hesitant. He stays in the same rhythmic pattern regardless of the relative importance of the shot in terms of the competitive situation that exists. It is my contention that if you were to film Littler's swing on the first hole of a practice round and again on the final and deciding hole of a major tournament, you would have to label them to tell which was which.

To describe Littler's grip, stance, and posture would be merely to repeat what the game's best theorists describe as correct. He waggles the club in just the smooth and unhurried tempo to be maintained in the swing, and from this waggle he seems to flow into the start of the backswing. Fortunately for the observer seeking to get a clear mental picture of the correct moves, Gene's is a relatively slow tempo in contrast with other fine golfers with fine swings who move a bit too fast for the average observer to take in all of what is happening.

Perhaps more than any other golfer on the current scene, he moves the club back in what has come to be known as "one piece," meaning that the hands, arms, shoulders, and hips seem to move in complete unison. Many experts would describe this initial backswing move as the outstanding feature of the Littler swing, but the rest of it is so classically right that one must make a very fine distinction to say that any one phase is outstanding.

Different golfers tend to emphasize—maybe even exaggerate—the relative importance of different phases of the swing as keys to a good overall swing. Australian Peter Thomson and Jack Nicklaus, for instance, are strong on a smooth and unhurried takeaway straight back away from the ball as a means of ensuring that the rest of the swing will go well. Hogan, especially, sees staying on a correct and repeating backswing plane as being of transcendent importance. The value of a full shoulder-turn going back is generally stressed in expert circles. I'm satisfied that nobody would criticize Littler on any of these points.

Gene Littler just before impact—the crucial moment.

Also, it is universally recognized that the hips should lead the downswing and that there must be no hint of hitting from the top with any premature action of the hands. Here again Littler would get the hearty approbation of any critic.

It hardly needs saying that the rest of Littler's downswing is in the classic mold—the delayed uncocking of the wrists, the clubhead accelerating through the hitting area of the swing, and all that. These things stem naturally from the correctness of the moves preceding them. Littler becomes, as Hogan put it, the "captive" of his own good swing.

I have included with this text a picture showing the one thing that I think keeps Littler's swing from being completely beyond criticism. It is that his leg stiffens just enough at impact to keep him from realizing his maximum power. I think that if the left knee remained flexed more as he moves through the ball, he would hit his drives, some 10 yards or so farther. And just a slightly longer-hitting Littler would be even tougher to beat than he already is—which, I hasten to add, is very tough indeed.

To fill out the portrait of Littler the golfer, it should be added that he is one of the game's best strategists. Few if any of his contemporaries play a course more intelligently than he does. He plays well within himself, so to speak, and you can watch him play many rounds without seeing him take a risk that is not fully warranted. He just goes along and executes those good shots with that fine swing and lets the results take care of themselves. In this general connection, the nickname of "Gene the Machine" is one of the most apt on the tour.

There are some who say that Littler would win more often than he does if he pushed himself more—if he could lift himself to greater heights of effort and inspiration, in the Palmer tradition. Maybe so. But I think Littler himself would know more about that than anyone else. And anyway, that type of player wouldn't be Littler. The fact that Littler returned to winning form soon after his illness proves that he is not lacking in inner strength and fortitude.

A Player's Gallery

The photographs accompanying this section are intended to illustrate some important facts about the golf swing. Chief among them is that whatever dissimilarities are apparent in certain phases of the swings of fine players, they are remarkably similar in that critical segment called the impact area. Perhaps the basic message to be conveyed is that it doesn't matter by what route the player reaches a correct position just before clubhead and ball collide so long as he reaches it (a point that has already been made and is in fact elementary).

There is, to be sure, a generally standardized method of starting the club back and getting it to the top of the back-swing, as described in detail by Bobby Jones, Ben Hogan, Jack Nicklaus, and just about every other expert whose views on golf have reached print. What they have said on the subject, however, is what is essentially correct for them individually—and, because they were or are orthodox swingers as well as very good swingers, it may logically be assumed that their methods would work well for the vast majority of golfers. But there are, as we shall see, some strong exceptions. However, the learning golfer should not assume from these exceptions that any sort of technique will do for the backswing. This is far from the case. He should learn the standard method, while being aware that some personal modifications are permissible and may even be helpful.

A "good" golf swing, then, is one that brings the player and his club into the correct hitting position as shown in the photographs of Bob Lunn, Bert Yancey, Dan Sikes, Mason Rudolph, Johnny Pott, Bob Goalby, Lee Trevino, Don January, and Orville Moody. Their main feature in common is that the hands are nicely ahead of the trailing clubhead and the wrists are still to some degree cocked—or, to put it another way, and perhaps more precisely, the wrists are not fully uncocked. Another common feature is that the hips have turned out of the way to permit free passage of the arms and hands through the hitting area, allowing them to stay on the correct path as contrasted with blocking such passage and forcing these elements to bring the clubhead into the ball along some other and incorrect path—outside-in and across the ball, for instance.

Dave Marr, Gardner Dickinson, and Jerry Barber are caught at just about the very instant of impact.

Gary Player, Tony Jacklin, Bob Murphy, and Billy Maxwell are seen in the first stages of the follow-through, or post-impact, segment.

Miller Barber and Gay Brewer are shown in two different stages of the backswing. They are presented because both have been criticized as having odd, or even incorrect, backswings. I think a more apt adjective would be "distinctive," because while Barber and Brewer do indeed have quite a backswing loop (or, in Brewer's case, loops), their tour records certainly argue strongly against their backswing being incorrect.

For purposes of individual comment on each, the pictures are generally arranged in the order of the swing stage they depict.

One can imagine Miller Barber a few years ago writing a letter to a professional, enclosing a picture of himself in an early stage of his backswing and asking whether, in the pro's expert opinion, he should seek his fortune on the P.G.A. tour. Pursuing this purely fanciful situation a bit further, one can also imagine the pro answering with a horrified "Good Lord, No!" and later being embarrassed and considerably mystified as Barber began winning upwards of $100,000 a year on the tour. I'm afraid it might have happened that way with me, although I knew Barber to be a good player some two or three years before he actually did turn pro in 1958.

A few months ago, Barber said, "I know I look funny taking the club back, but my way works for me, and when I get into the hitting area I'm in as strong a position as anybody." I think that covers the subject as well as anything could. As is well-known, Barber had a good lead going into the final round of the 1969 U.S. Open at The Champions Club in Houston, having played three fine rounds on this demanding course before coming up with one of his rare bad rounds on the last day. Had he won, he might have written a book, as most U.S. Open winners do. It would have been interesting.

Obviously, Barber takes the clubhead back well outside the line, and not only does he have what is known as the flying right elbow, he also actually appears to get the right elbow out and away from the body as far as he can. Then, as he absolutely must to get in a tenable position for the start of the downswing, he loops the club and brings the right elbow in close to the body. It is in this maneuver that he goes from the extremely unorthodox to the orthodox.

It will be seen that Barber gets well into his backswing

Miller Barber going back into his loop.

Gay Brewer at the top of his backswing.

with no turn of the hips at all. The shoulders have begun to turn, and have indeed turned about as much as they can be turned without some turn of the hips. Thus we find him being orthodox in an unorthodox way. He is getting into a good turn of the shoulders while retarding the turn of the hips, winding up the body so as to facilitate leading the downswing with a strong unwinding of the hips—according to the Hogan prescription. The moral of the Barber story would seem to be that the backswing permits considerable latitude, but the downswing does not.

In recent years, Gay Brewer has had about as much television exposure as any golfer, besides having been seen first hand by big galleries in his banner years of 1967–68. Thus his is one of the better-known swings on the P.G.A. tour. He has also had considerable success in Great Britain.

The Brewer swing is distinguished by so much looping going back that he is known as the most prolific "skywriter" on the tour. Nevertheless, his final top-of-the-backswing position is basically good, as the picture shows. (He is shown hitting a 4-wood off the first tee in the Memphis Open. For a full drive he takes the club back farther, about to the point where the shaft would be horizontal.) His shoulder turn has put his back to the target, as is recommended, and his lesser turn of the hips gives him a good windup of the muscles to be used in the downswing. The clubhead is in the usually prescribed square position, or perhaps just slightly open. The right elbow is more out from the body than adherents of the classic swing would advocate, but just past this point in his swing he gets it back in to put himself in a good striking position.

Brewer has another swing peculiarity that is not nearly as noticeable as his looping backswing. With the start of the downswing the upper part of the body moves in the direction of the target—amounting almost to the sway that swing purists deplore—and he gives himself quite a task to make the clubhead catch up and be moving toward the target at impact. As much as any other player on the tour, Brewer gets a free-flowing release through the ball—what Bobby Jones called free-wheeling through impact. This is an effect that Brewer works to keep in his swing, and it helps to make him one of the more powerful hitters on the tour.

Into the Hitting Area

The pictures of Trevino, Rudolph, Pott, January, Yancey, Goalby, and Sikes offer a good study of basically similar positions in slightly varying stages of the downswing. There are, of course, a number of surface differences as well as points in common.

In each instance the left hip has turned out of the way and the hips have moved well forward of the position at the top of the backswing. The right elbow is tucked in close to the body and just forward of the right hip. With the exception of Goalby, each player's left arm has remained fully extended, straight but not rigid. Goalby's left arm is distinctly bent at this critical stage of the swing, reflecting, I'm sure, something that went slightly awry in an earlier stage of the swing. For several weeks prior to the time these pictures were taken, Goalby had not been playing up to his usual standard, and this bending of the left arm may well have been a key to his problem. It is axiomatic that one of the arms should be fully extended throughout the swing, which is another way of saying that the left arm should be straight until, in the follow-through, the right arm straightens and the left arm begins to fold in much as the right arm does on the backswing.

As a group, these pictures show the extent to which the clubhead should trail the hands through the hitting area. This is much the same as saying that a good swing necessarily embodies a delayed uncocking of the wrists—a delayed hit.

Bob Goalby

Dan Sikes

Lee Trevino

Johnny Pott

Bert Yancey

Don January

Mason Rudolph

This principle is best exemplified—you could even say exaggeratedly so—by Sikes. If you study the picture of Sikes (hitting a short iron), you have to wonder how he can possibly get the clubface square at impact. The answer has to be that he is very strong and very quick with his hands. Part of the explanation lies in the fact that Sikes's normal shot pattern is right to left. It is inevitable that this shot would start out to the right of the target and only super-quick hand action could give it the spin to come back on target.

Trevino, of course, appears to violate certain principles of the classic swing, notably that the back should be generally straight, bent only slightly from the trunk. Trevino is a shut-faced player and swings in a flatter plane than most, both of which features contribute to the fact that he is a low-ball hitter—which led him to say that the Augusta National course (scene of the Masters) was not for him. I have heard it said of Trevino that he gets a lot of fine golf out of a bad swing. I would call this a superficial assessment of his swing. From the hips down, particularly, he is a very good swinger.

The close observer will note in these pictures varying degrees of what is called aggressiveness. In Pott, for instance, you can readily see his tremendous power building up to almost literally explode into the ball at impact. By contrast, it is manifest that Yancey works more toward maintaining a good, smooth tempo. January is also strongly aggressive through the hitting area. He has an exceptionally long backswing, dropping the club well below the horizontal at the top. This adds something to the problem of timing the swing, but as the picture makes clear, January solves it.

I would say Rudolph's position entering the hitting area is in all respects sound, but a bit more flex in the left knee would give him a stronger lateral movement of the lower body through the impact area, with a consequent increase in power.

At Impact

When the accompanying picture of Orville Moody was made, he was two weeks away from becoming the 1969 Open champion. As far as we know he was the choice of only one expert to win that tournament. The prophet was Lee Trevino, who must have discerned in Moody's swing what is apparent in the photograph showing him a minute fraction of a second away from impact—that he has the sound, powerful swing calculated to get the distance and accuracy necessary on a U.S. Open course.

I'm sure Ben Hogan would be particularly high on Moody's swing because he so clearly arches (supinates) the left wrist through impact. Hogan considers this essential to a truly effect swing. In effect, arching the left wrist through impact keeps the clubface square to the ball an instant longer than does a release through the ball that lacks this movement. It also slightly lessens the effective loft of the club while at the same time maintaining the square clubface position. Thus it is a highly valuable aid to accuracy on all shots, and on iron shots in particular it helps by adding distance without any loss of the backspin needed to brake the shot when it hits the green.

I think the wrist position is what first catches the expert eye on seeing Moody at impact. Further observation reveals virtually nothing to be critical about. A true perfectionist probably would want to see the left foot planted a bit more firmly on the ground (the heel appears to be up just slightly), but Moody's is certainly an excellent position overall.

In Bob Lunn's position at impact we see just about all of the fine attributes that characterize Moody's, lacking only the supination feature. Lunn, who hits long and towering tee shots in the Jack Nicklaus pattern, moves through the ball

Orville Moody

Bob Lunn at impact

with the back of the left hand square to the target and the wrist straight rather than arched. In my view this left-wrist position is of itself as good as the supinated one, with the advantage of the latter being that it keeps the clubface aligned squarely for a slightly longer period and hence provides a greater margin of safety.

With Jerry Barber we get a quite different picture. It is clear that he started with the left hand in an especially strong position—at least three knuckles visible and the thumb and forefinger V pointing to the right shoulder. With this position of the left hand, Barber cannot release through the ball as Moody and Lunn do, putting the back of the left hand to the target. Such a release with the Barber grip would just about close the clubface completely, sending the ball off very much to the left and very low, perhaps not even airborne. Thus Barber has to use a different type of release, sort of under and up, pronating the left hand instead of supinating it as Moody does, and as Hogan so strongly recommends.

Barber, a veteran whose tournament appearances are rare nowadays, learned his golf back when the strongly positioned left hand was part of the accepted way of gripping the club, and he did not see fit to make so drastic a change in his game when the so-called modern grip came into popular use. He was, however, a quite successful player well into the modern era and won the P.G.A. in 1961 against a field made up largely of younger, stronger, and considerably larger players. He achieved his success mainly through a superb short game, but actually he was by no means a short hitter, particularly in light of his small stature.

Two contrasting styles and how they work through impact are seen in Dave Marr and Gardner Dickinson. Marr is one of the true stylists among current players, a golfer who sticks closely to the established fundamentals and tends to concentrate on maintaining a smooth tempo. The contrast between him and Dickinson in the hitting segment of the swing conveys my idea of the term "aggressiveness" as it applies to the

CARY MIDDLECOFF

Jerry Barber

Dave Marr

golf swing. Marr is by no means passive, but you can see in him the controlled movement that distinguishes the swinger from the hitter.

Probably more than any other player in the top rank of golf, Dickinson moves and keeps moving the lower part of his body to help him add power to his swing. The observer is bound to notice that Dickinson has a decided dip coming into the ball—more so than Byron Nelson had. There are those who would characterize this dip in Dickinson's swing as a flaw, but actually it works to his advantage by giving him an exceptionally strong lateral thrust on the downswing.

Post Impact

By the time a good golfer reaches the stage of the swing shown in the pictures of Gary Player, Tony Jacklin, Bob Murphy, and Billy Maxwell, the ball is some 15 yards on its way and traveling at 100 miles an hour or more. Thus if you look at it from a purely practical point of view it doesn't make any difference whether the player's post-impact position is like Player's, for instance, or flat on his face on the ground. But to look at it this way is to lose sight of the vital fact that the whole swing—and that, of course, includes the post-impact position—should be thought out in advance. The post-impact position clearly reflects whether it is part of a good swing or a bad one.

It should be programmed into the swing that after the club-head is a foot or so past where the ball was, both arms should be fully extended. It is the only place in the swing where this correctly happens. All four of the players pictured just after impact reach this position very much as prescribed. And, as goes without saying among the best players, the head is where it was when the swing started. Of the four pictured in this stage of the swing, Bob Murphy would appear to get the

Gardner Dickinson

Gary Player

Bob Murphy just after impact

Tony Jacklin

Billy Maxwell

fullest extension through the ball. It is no mean feat to reach the position Murphy is shown in without having rolled the right hand over and past the left. Jacklin, for example, is about half as far past the ball's original position as Murphy, and his right hand has begun to pass the left, as happens in the normal release.

There are two descriptive phrases about this stage of the golf swing—or rather what the player's position at this stage reflects as to what went on through the hitting area. One is that he "stayed with the shot"; the other is that he "came off the shot." It could not be said of any of the players pictured that he came off the shot, but it could be said of Murphy that he stays with the shot exceptionally well—beautifully.

Maxwell's position leaves itself open to some criticism. The fact that both heels are well up off the ground at this stage is clear evidence that some of the power potentially available through the lower part of the body has been dissipated. Also, the straightness and partial rigidity of Maxwell's left leg through impact indicates that he does not move through the ball as aggressively as (in strong contrast) Player does.

As is well-known to close followers of the tour, Maxwell is probably the shortest hitter among the consistent money-winners. His forte is accuracy combined with masterful use of the short irons—the 8-iron down through the wedge. Maxwell is more fully aware than anybody that he has to have a superior short game to compete successfully against his longer-hitting competition. He is a prime example of a player who extracts maximum results from the skills available to him. As such he offers an excellent example of what can be accomplished through full utilization of superior short-game skills to compensate for a shortage of power.

Some Personal Conclusions

I would advise the aspiring golfer to carefully assess the discrepancies and apparent contradictions cited in this book regarding the golf-swing theories of the great players from Vardon to Jack Nicklaus. Only in the case of Vardon's holding that the right leg should stiffen at the end of the backswing and the left leg likewise at impact would I say positively that subsequent theory and practice have proven otherwise. I think that the techniques of all successful modern players much more nearly support Ben Hogan's theory that the knees should remain flexed throughout the swing to the same degree as in address.

As has been indicated, the stated theories of Hogan and Palmer as to keeping the head still are by no means mutually incompatible. You will remember that Hogan says that in a good swing—one in which the body movements are correctly carried out—the head automatically stays in place, and Palmer says that if the head is kept still the correct body movements will essentially execute themselves as they should. Here, as so often happens in golf, we have two authorities saying much the same thing but differing as to which is cause and which effect.

Just about any golfer can easily prove the above point to himself. Let him merely test the proposition with the shortest and simplest of golf swings—the putt—by trying to keep the head still on every putting stroke for 18 holes. Firstly, I think he will be unable to keep his head still on every putt for an entire round. Secondly—and more germane to the question at hand—I think he will note that when he makes a good stroke the head will remain in place, and vice versa. Thirdly, I think he will recognize that the two things go together to the point of being inseparable, both as to theory and practice—and that, by simple extension, the same thing applies fully to the longer swings.

To a vast majority of golfers, I'm sure, it would appear to be a simple thing to rivet the eyes on the back of the ball and keep them there until the ball is hit and on its way to the target, thus insuring that the head does not move. In fact, a number of highly regarded teachers—Alex Morrison, to cite perhaps the most notable—have urged that the player not only keep his eyes on the ball until impact but also on the spot where the ball was for a prescribed number of seconds. I can only offer the opinion that this advice is basically sound to the extent that the player is able to follow it. When he fails, he may be quite exasperated with himself, on the grounds that what he was trying to do and did not was absurdly simple. It is not.

Any one of a number of faulty moves in the pre-hit stages of the swing will force a movement of the head, which in turn will pull the eyes off the back of the ball. Similarly, moving the head so that the eyes can no longer focus on the ball may precede (and cause) a faulty swing movement.

Actually, the whole thing can be likened to the question of the priority of the chicken or the egg.

Much the same reasoning can be applied to the theory of the backswing—the wrongness of the flying right elbow and so on. Here I would empasize again that the purpose of the backswing is to put the player in the best (for him) striking position, plus setting up a good swing rhythm. If the elbow "wanders" (to borrow a term that Bernard Darwin applied to Vardon), it is of no overriding consequence, provided the elbow gets back on the right track at the critical instant, which comes partway through the downswing. A "correct" backswing, then, is neither more nor less than one that leads to a correct position as the player enters the hitting area. One backswing is better than another to the degree that it engenders a downswing calculated to consistently produce accurate and powerful shots. It follows from this that an uncomplicated backswing is most correct and desirable, as the mere fact of its being uncomplicated makes it easier to duplicate on successive swings. That is the basic idea.

To make my next point I would like to put in a chunk of personal experience and elaborate on Hogan's dictum that "golf is a game of constant correction." When in the early spring of 1947 I joined the P.G.A. tour I was twenty-six years old and had behind me some sixteen years as a golfer of vast enthusiasm and great earnestness. I brought to this new and ambitious endeavor a golf swing from whose basic principles I have never departed. As to what those basic principles are, I think I need only say that they are orthodox—not different enough from what is now considered basically sound to warrant a separate description. I was, of course, unique on the tour in that I came to a complete stop at the top of the backswing and paused for a full second or more before launching into the downswing. But this I then regarded—and still do, although it has virtually disappeared from my swing—as a personal modification not necessarily applicable to or desirable for anyone else.

I knew it was a good swing and was firmly resolved not to change it basically—only to improve it. The improvement I hoped for was in making the swing repeat itself more consistently—to reach the point where each swing was my best swing. I thought this was both possible and feasible. Like just about every other golfer that I know of, I saw no reason why if my swing worked well one day I could not make it work as well or better on the next and subsequent days.

It was in pursuit of this ideal that I learned to my disappointment that the game is indeed one of constant correction. Even the best of players on their best days cannot produce the best swing they are capable of more than three or four times in a single 18-hole round. Hogan said that on a given day one or two of his shots—seldom more—would come off exactly as planned.

The attainable golf-swing ideal, then, is to develop one that will produce a number of good, serviceable shots per round and the barest possible minimum of really bad shots—shots than can result in the loss of more than one stroke on a hole (this is what is meant by "keeping the ball in play"). If the golfer accepts this line of reasoning, as I rather quickly did, he will have come to a good understanding of the basic strategy of the game, which is that you have to accommodate your thinking to the demands and perils of the course. I think the best way to make the point clear is through a couple of examples. Take the justly famous No. 10 hole at the Augusta National, for instance. The ideal drive on this par-4 hole is down the left side of the fairway with a bit of a tail-hook (or draw) on it. Such a drive figures to land on a down-slope and roll enough to leave the player with a second shot of some 150–160 yards from the best possible angle to the green —a simple 6- or 7-iron ordinarily. A drive hit equally hard down the right side of the fairway will hit on level ground and get little roll—adding 50 or more yards to the effective length of the hole. Naturally, as is consonant with the principles of a good golf hole, the attempt to reach the ideal position is fraught with danger. Just a few yards to the left of this ideal position are those towering pines and flowering dogwoods, which are beautiful only if they do not block your line to the hole. So the question the player must ask himself before hitting his tee shot is how much of a chance is he willing to take. The answer lies not only in how good the player is (or thinks he is) but in how his golf swing is currently functioning. If he is driving well that day, and particularly if his normal swing produces a slight hook or draw, he may confidently aim for what is sometimes called "Position A." If, however, his hooks and draws tend to get a bit out of hand—either habitually or on this particular day—he will want to play for the center of the fairway, preferring to have a slightly longer and harder second shot over risking too much on a chancy tee shot.

On this same hole, with the pin placed on the right side of the green, a slight fade on the second shot offers the best chance to get close to the pin—but a slight overfade will end up in the big sand bunker to the right. So again the player must think strategically in terms of how his swing figures to work at the time.

All this would seem to fall into the category of golf strategy rather than of the golf swing. But the fact is that a good golf swing is to a considerable degree dependent on good golf strategy. It is indeed conducive to a good swing to have the mind clear and resting easily on the knowledge that a sound plan has been formed for the shot that the swing is being called on to produce. Putting it another way, the player should not only try to develop as good a swing as possible from a technical standpoint, he should also get to know and understand that swing. If the player places unwarranted demands on his swing—such as pressing too hard for extra distance—the swing will be apt to break down under the strain. The simplest illustration of the point lies in the age-old admonition "Don't try to kill the ball." From the beginning, writers on golf stressed that the swing must be a thing of controlled power, even though maximum distance was the primary objective. And later on, when Palmer and others urged the player to "hit it hard," they certainly didn't mean that such golf-swing essentials as staying on balance and maintaining rhythm should be forgotten or ignored.

I think that the great advantage both aspiring golfers and teachers of today have over those of a generation ago is the learner's opportunity to study the techniques of the game's best players, on television or in person, and thus get a better understanding of such subtle points as how hard to try to hit the ball. It has always been difficult to put into words just what a good golf swing is. A teacher can tell a pupil that, for instance, he mustn't wreck his balance and timing by trying to swing too hard, whereupon the pupil starts swinging too easy, which is also an enemy of balance and timing. But if this pupil can watch, say, Gene Littler swing, he can sense immediately what his teacher had in mind.

Along this same line, if an aspiring player were to model himself on Arnold Palmer and knew about him only through reading and hearsay, he could easily get the impression that Palmer always swung with all his might, always went straight for the pin regardless of the possible consequences, and banged every putt for the back of the cup. But if he coupled his secondhand knowledge with observing Palmer in action, he would see immediately that although Palmer does swing a little harder than most and does play a little bolder than most, the difference is in degree only—and slight degree at that.

Hand-Action, Wrist-Snap and Such

I think that from the beginning I had a reasonably clear idea of the correct function of the hands and wrists in the golf swing. Emmett Spicer, on whose excellent and powerful golf swing I basically modeled my own, certainly used his hands and wrists correctly. And before I joined the tour I was privileged to play with many fine and knowledgeable golfers, notably Bobby Jones and Ben Hogan. During my years on the tour, I naturally played mostly with very good golfers—golfers who not only played well but were thoroughly grounded in the theory of the swing. So it was after I largely quit playing competitive golf that I got to play and talk the game with sizable numbers of those known, for want of a better term, as average golfers. It was something of a surprise for me, then, to learn how many golfers conceived of hand-action and wrist-snap in a way that could with considerable accuracy be described as backward. I had, of course, often heard nonexpert golfers attribute a certain player's extraordinary power to a "wrist-snap" or to great "hand-action," but it never really occurred to me that a lot of them meant that the secret of power was to snap the clubhead forward in the hitting area so that it passed the hands moving into the ball. Later—and more particularly in preparing to write this book—I found out that they did in fact mean that.

Such an action of the hands and wrists (they necessarily work together, of course), far from adding power, considerably subtracts it. It takes away some of that power the hands and wrists supply in a correct swing. Also, in order for the hands and wrists to send the clubhead into the ball ahead of themselves at impact, the lower part of the body has to slow down—has to be braked, so to speak—which also causes a power loss—quite a large power loss in fact.

It is by no means clear how such a theory of golf-swing mechanics became prevalent. As we have seen, Harry Vardon deplored any conscious wrist-snap as a means of adding power. It was Vardon's view that in a correct swing the hands and wrists would "take care of themselves." At any rate, he advised against using the wrist to snap the clubhead forward, and he expressed this view around the turn of the century— at a time when golfers everywhere considered Vardon preeminent, both as player and theorist. Yet the error persisted, and to a surprising extent it still does. (Ernest Jones, with his emphasis on manipulating the clubhead solely with the hands, doubtless had an effect in this matter, as did Tommy Armour with his presentation of the role played by the wrists and hands.)

The action that sends the clubhead ahead of the hands at impact has come to be called pronation. It was Ben Hogan who so strongly made the point that pronation in the hitting area was exactly what the player does not want, and that what he does want is pronation's opposite—supination.

> At impact, said Hogan, "the back of the left hand faces toward your target. The wristbone is definitely raised. It points to the target and, at the moment the ball is contacted, it is out in front, nearer to the target than any other part of the hand. When the left wrist is in this position, the left hand will not check or interrupt the speed with which your clubhead is traveling. There's no danger either that the right hand will overpower the left and twist the club over. It can't. . . .
>
> Every good golfer has his left wrist in this supinating position at impact. Every poor golfer does the exact reverse. As his club comes into the ball, he starts to pronate the left wrist—to turn it so that the palm will be facing down.
>
> When a golfer's left wrist begins to pronate just before impact, it changes his arc: it shortens it drastically and makes the pitch of his upswing altogether too steep and constricted. At the very point in the swing in which he should be increasing the speed of his hands, by pronating he slows them down. . . .

The British scientific team described an impact position with the clubhead ahead of the hands as "weak" and a position with the hands slightly ahead of the clubhead as "strong." This was their way of saying that pronation is wrong and supination right.

A majority of modern experts would probably say that at impact the back of the left hand should be facing along the target line and that the left arm and the club should form a straight, or unbroken, line from the left shoulder to the club-head. This figures out to be neither supination nor pronation. A number of very good players do in fact supinate the left wrist at impact, but not as a conscious or programmed part of their swings. They simply do it by virtue of having worked out what to them feels right in a good swing, and unlike Hogan, have never brought their concept of the impact position to so fine a point.

Therein lies yet another illustration of the fact that many golf-swing movements are naturally and inevitably tied in with others—are reciprocal, so to speak—and attempts to consider them separately can lead to confusion. Our old friend Ike S. Handy comes readily to mind in this connection. When he said that the player should swing the top of the club (or swing his hands) rather than swing the clubhead, he was—in his own way—saying "do not pronate the left wrist at impact."

In years to come, perhaps the theory of hitting a golf ball will be drastically revised. If so, I thing that among the essential features of the "new swing" will be keeping both knees flexed to the same degree throughout and making very sure that the clubhead never passes ahead of the hands until after impact. It may even happen that somebody will figure out a simple and readily understandable way of describing the correct golf swing. But then, that might take away much of the game's appeal.

Among the leading golf theorists who set down their views in writing, Ben Hogan stands out as the one who described the grip with the greatest exactness and attention to detail. In his *Modern Fundamentals of Golf*, Hogan gave as much space to the grip as to the stance, backswing, and downswing. Much of what he said about the grip is in line with the theories of other modern experts. But he added one detail that, according to my research, is his alone:

To promote a right-hand grip that is strong where it should be strong (and which will then more than offset the dangerous tendency to let the tips of thumb and forefinger work like a pincer), I recommend the golfer-reader to cultivate the following habit: School yourself when you are taking your grip so that the thumb and the adjoining part of the hand across the V—the part that is the upper extension of the forefinger—press up against each other tightly, as inseparable as Siamese twins. Keep them pressed together as you begin to affix your grip, and maintain this airtight pressure between them when you fold the right hand over the left thumb. In this connection, I like to feel that the knuckle on the back of my right hand above the forefinger is pressing to the left, toward my target. It rides almost on top of the shaft. I know then that the club has to be in my fingers. Furthermore, when you fold the right hand over the left thumb—and there is a lot left to fold over—the left thumb will fit perfectly in the "cup" formed in the palm of your folded right hand. They fit together like pieces in a jigsaw puzzle.

On the P.G.A. tour today, as well as in amateur competition at the highest level, the grip in general use could with considerable accuracy be called the "Hogan grip," at least with regard to its distinguishing feature, which is the left hand turned much more to the left than was thought practicable in the earlier days of the game. It is, of course, a matter of pure necessity to have the left hand positioned basically as Hogan advocates if the hands are to move effectively through the hitting area without some pronation. The golfer can easily prove the point to himself by gripping the club with three knuckles of the left hand showing and the V's formed by the thumb and forefinger of each hand pointing to the right shoulder, as was considered standard in the past, and then trying to hit the ball with the back of the left hand facing along the intended line of flight. Such a procedure would leave the clubface turned well inward (to the left) at impact, and much of the effective loft of the club would be eliminated.

The reader may have noted that the one major point on which the British researchers disagree with Hogan is the need for preciseness and exactness in gripping the club. This group, as noted, takes the view that, within limits, a particular gripping method can be right for one player and not for another, due to individual anatomical variations and differences in the feel of the hands on the club. Personally, I think that in most instances where Hogan differs from other golf-swing theorists, the probable reason is that he theorized on a higher, more rarefied plane. With Hogan a thing is either right or wrong, and never mind what is approximately right or what would adequately serve for golfers in the bulk.

In the above connection it seems likely that some of Tommy Armour's expressed theories were aimed at helping the average golfer improve his game rather than at what is ideal for a player who works at the game for a living and competes on the very highest level. Armour was, after all, basically a teacher by the time he got around to writing about the golf swing, and it seems a fair assumption that he saw no merit in burdening a pupil with something that might confuse rather than help.

Unfortunately, it seems unlikely that Hogan will again set forth his swing theories in book form. He once declared to a friend that never again would he write any instructional material. According to the friend, he kept getting letters from readers asking him to clarify certain points in his most recent book, and many of the questions contained in the letters revealed that the writer hadn't the slightest idea of what Hogan had tried to say in the book—and lacked the background to understand a technical explanation from the author. Hogan had tried very hard to make his points crystal clear, and it must have saddened and discouraged him to find himself not much better understood than, for instance, the early Einstein.

The fact is that any writer of golf instruction (myself certainly included) is bound to recognize the difficulty of getting his points across to the reader. The same goes for the teaching professional with his pupil right there with him, making it possible to demonstrate his points as he makes them. And perhaps the hardest point of all to make is that the correctness of the grip, which to the uninitiated can seem almost inconsequential, is in fact vital. So many golfers do not relate their bad shots to a basically bad grip, or to slight but relevant changes in their grip from one shot to the next. The errant player may have, for instance, moved his head or lost his balance and never suspect that a bad grip was the cause of the error.

The concept of the correct stance has not yet become standardized, nor, in my opinion, is it ever apt to be. No highly successful golfer of the present that I know of stands with his feet as close together as Bobby Jones did—except maybe Miller Barber. Nor does any current star stand to the ball with his feet spread as far apart as Walter Hagen did— with the possible exception of Doug Sanders. (I would be inclined to describe Sanders and Barber as certainly among the more unorthodox players of the modern era.)

Hogan, whom we seem always to get back to in the discussion of any phase of the golf swing, quite positively stated that a truly effective stance embodied keeping the upper arms quite close to and pressed against the sides of the chest. He also stoutly advocated bringing the elbows in as close to each other as is possible without undue strain. Few golfers, even among the pros, hew exactly to these principles of the stance. Gardner Dickinson does—in fact he hews to all of Hogan's principles. But Jay Hebert, whose success on the tour has been considerable, goes against these two particular Hogan stance principles. There always seems to be at least partial exceptions to any stated principle of the golf swing.

There is, however, virtually unanimous conformity among good golfers in standing to the ball in a generally upright, nonslouching position. It is a matter of logic that the arms and hands should have ample room to move freely into and through the hitting area, which presupposes that the player's back will be held generally straight and that his posterior will protrude to the rear somewhat as if he were about to sit down on a high stool. (The point, obviously, applies less to skinny golfers than to those with ample stomachs.)

Our best present-day golfers do not make a big point of squaring the right foot at an exact right angle with the intended line of flight, thus ensuring that the hips do not turn even slightly more than they should on the backswing. Neither do they turn the left foot outward to any precise degree—a quarter of a turn, or some 22 degrees, as Hogan prescribed. But you rarely, if ever, see a good player stand with his right toe pointed out to facilitate a full turn of the hips on the backswing, as Vardon and Jones both did and advocated. Today's best players may not be emulating Hogan consciously, but his influence is nonetheless having its effect.

Seemingly different theories abound as to the manner and method of triggering the start of the backswing. One great player may say, as Julius Boros has, that you merely start the left shoulder turning around to the right and the rest of the backswing components fall naturally and easily into place. Another player of roughly equal stature may say that you should move into this critical stage of the swing with a turning of the hips, or of the right shoulder, or a pushing off with the inside of the left foot, or any of a bewildering number of other initiating movements. The point to remember is that such bits of advice do not necessarily (or even usually) contradict one another. They are more often different ways of saying much the same thing.

A golfer may actually play beautifully during a given week and win an important championship and afterward truthfully say that it was all due to some small gimmick that he had never used before, like starting the clubhead back outside the line and bringing the right elbow back in at the start of the downswing—or some similar movement. Then, in the following tournament, he might play badly and scarcely remember the gimmicky movement to which he had attributed his prior week's success. It often works that way.

As to the downswing, the main problem is one that most golfers, however talented, have in common. It is to find a reliable and consistent way to avoid starting the downward movement with the hands. To put it another way, the problem is to achieve a delayed action of the hands—a delayed hit. The downswing-initiating movements chiefly advocated include a turning of the left hip back around to the left, a shifting of the weight back over to the left side, a downward tugging movement with the left arm, and a pushing-off with the inside of the right foot. As we have seen, any one of these movements is calculated to produce the others, to a large degree, automatically and simultaneously. The student of the swing may want to experiment with each of these movements.

In any event, it should be remembered that whatever down-swing-triggering movement is used, that is the last movement of the swing the player can carry out consciously and in full awareness of what is happening. The rest of the swing will be, as Jack Nicklaus describes it, a reflex action.

Looking back over this text it strikes me that the main thought I would like to leave with the reader is the one expressed above—that the downswing is in fact almost wholly a reflex action, that what happens after the downswing is launched has been determined by what has gone before. I think that if the student of the swing is clear on this point, his learning process can be speeded up and made more effective. I consider this point—one that has not been sufficiently emphasized in the past—vital to a real understanding of the swing process. The student must, of course, know what should happen in an effective downswing, but at the same time he should be aware that he can't effectively alter it once he is fully into it.